Aspects
of
LOVE

Aspects
of
LOVE

An Exploration of
1 Corinthians 13

J. BARRIE SHEPHERD

UPPER
ROOM BOOKS
Nashville

ASPECTS OF LOVE
Copyright © 1995 by J. Barrie Shepherd
All rights reserved.

Scripture quotations not otherwise identified are from the New Revised Standard Version of the Bible, copyright 1989 by the Division of Christian Education of the National Council of the Churches of Christ in the USA and are used by permission.

Scripture quotations designated RSV are from the Revised Standard Version of the Bible, copyrighted 1946, 1952, and © 1971 by the Division of Christian Education, National Council of the Churches of Christ in the USA. Used by permission.

Scripture quotations designated KJV are from the King James Version of the Bible.

Cover design: Gore Studio, Inc.
First Printing: November 1995 (5)
ISBN: 0-8358-0764-9
Library of Congress Catalog Card Number: 95-78717

Printed in the United States of America

To Mhairi

*who has taught me more of love
than I could ever learn.*

ALSO BY J. BARRIE SHEPHERD

Faces at the Cross
(A Lent and Easter Collection of Poetry and Prose)

Faces at the Manger
(An Advent-Christmas Sampler of Poems,
Prayers, and Meditations)

Seeing with the Soul
(Daily Meditations on the Parables of Jesus in Luke)

The Moveable Feast
(Selected Poems for the Christian Year and Beyond)

A Pilgrim's Way
(Meditations for Lent and Easter)

A Child Is Born
(Meditations for Advent and Christmas)

Praying the Psalms
(Daily Meditations on Cherished Psalms)

Prayers from the Mount
(Daily Meditations on The Sermon on the Mount)

Encounters
(Poetic Meditations on the Old Testament)

A Diary of Prayer
(Daily Meditations on the Parables of Jesus)

Diary of Daily Prayer

CONTENTS

———— ✠ ————

Preface

sk any about-to-be-married couple what scripture verses they would like read at their wedding, and in nine cases out of ten, they will select 1 Corinthians 13. A philosophical few may choose Ecclesiastes 3 with its "time for every matter under heaven: a time to be born, and a time to die." There is even the occasional, foolhardy male who elects what I call the "kamikaze approach" and proposes Ephesians chapter five, "Wives, submit yourselves unto your own husbands, as unto the Lord," KJV. But for most, it is that "bit about love in Corinthians"—1 Corinthians 13—"and the greatest of these is love."

There is little to wonder about in this choice, since this is one of the most evocative and moving passages in all of literature. However, the chief problem with a passage like 1 Corinthians 13 is that—like the Lord's Prayer or Psalm 23—it becomes so beloved, so revered, so much a part of the traditional trappings that people begin to hear it without listening. They become so caught up and comforted by the sound of these reassuring syllables that they are no longer capable of catching the message of the actual words. Thus they miss out on much of the wonder and power of Paul's insights for the marriage bond as well as for all other human relationships.

In the following chapters, I will attempt to peel away the layers of custom and familiarity, to permit these living words and phrases to speak, as if for the first time, to the heart of that experience we know and yet do not know, we grasp and yet reach out for, the experience of love.

This experience is one of the holiest, and at the same time the most human, elements of existence. It should be entered into with prayer. It should be pounced upon with glee. It should be handled with reverence. It should be savored with delight. Needless to say, love is a paradox. If these pages can illuminate that paradox—for they will never resolve it—then my prayers will be answered and my delight will be full.

The scholarship and insights of many who have trod the path ahead of me have aided and informed my preparation of this book. In particular I wish to acknowledge the work of William Barclay, the great Scottish New Testament scholar and interpreter. I also treasure the work of Henry Drummond, whose slender volume *The Greatest Thing in the World* is a devotional classic.

1

A Communications Crisis

━━━━━━━━━━━━━━━━━━━━━━━━━━━━━ ✛

*If I speak in the tongues of mortals and of angels,
but do not have love, I am a noisy gong or a
clanging cymbal.*

he tongues of mortals and of angels. What a
glorious way to begin! The phrase sings on
the lips, resounds in the ear, stirs magic in the
mind. It is a phrase that works, that achieves
what it sets out to achieve. And it works so well because
it bears so well the meaning it is trying to convey.

Paul is writing here of eloquence, of that rare gift of communicating ideas, proposals, possibilities—yes, and lies, slanders, half-truths too—but communicating them in such an effective way that the very sound of the words, let alone their content, brings about persuasion, wins the hearer over.

. . . the tongues of mortals and of angels . . .

Paul, of course, had specific tongues in mind. He wrote this letter, this First Epistle to the Corinthians, to a church torn apart; to a young, virtually newborn Christian congregation that had tragically split into feuds and factions over the whole business of speaking in tongues. Alien tongues these were, foreign, unintelligible, bizarre, seemingly spirit-possessed tongues.

This same phenomenon is alive within the church today. And regrettably, it is still a phenomenon that divides the family of faith. It splits churches into those who have the gift and those who do not; those who are privy to these arcane utterances and those who are shut out.

But beyond the specifics of this Corinthian church, beyond the age-old controversy over "speaking in tongues" and other such Pentecostal experiences, Paul's words bear a far more universal meaning. These "tongues of mortals and of angels" today also represent the tools, components, structural elements that make up what we call "communication."

And what an astounding era we live in for communication. The technology is so little short of miraculous it can take all one's time merely to keep up. While most people are still struggling to absorb the impact of computers, here come fax machines, cellular phones, satellite hook-ups, and even something astonishing called E- (for electronic) mail.

When my youngest daughter—the young are the ones who *can* cope with all this—graduated from high school, she told us of her classmates' plan to stay in touch. They simply type letters, announcements, updates, whatever onto the computer screens in their college dormitory rooms and Hey presto! (as the magicians said in the olden days), they are "networked" onto their classmates' screens across the country and, for all I know, the world. This is certainly the age of communications.

The irony is that despite the unparalleled means at our disposal, and an entire globe linked, networked to an inconceivable degree, we human beings are more divided, more parochial, more narrowly nationalistic, prejudiced, and violent toward one another than ever before.

People come to me as a pastor; they talk to me about the breakup of families, marriages, relationships, and repeatedly I hear the words—*communications failure*, *communications breakdown*. Yet these people, for the most part, communicate extremely well. It's not communications that have broken down but something much more basic.

We are living in a communications revolution, which is fast becoming a communications crisis. We have every means of communication imaginable, yet little of worth to communicate. Paul Tournier, the Swiss psychotherapist has written, "Listen to all the conversations of our world, between nations as well as between individuals. They are, for the most part, dialogues of the deaf."

As I read these words I see myself a child in Scotland, turning the dial on our old vacuum-tube radio, pulling in all the Babel voices of the continent of Europe and comprehending not one single word.

If I speak in the tongues of mortals and of angels, but do not have love, I am a noisy gong or a clanging cymbal.

What then is this love that Paul sees as essential; this love without which communication becomes null and void, a clanging, clashing din? As Cole Porter put it sixty years ago and more, "What is this thing called love?"

It has to be more than romantic love, that stuff the entertainment world elevates to the status of divinity. For all its exhilaration and fascination, that kind of love can give only a partial answer. Thomas Mann in *The Magic Mountain* described romantic love as "an intoxication by which one is possessed, under the influence of which one abhors nothing more than the thought of sobriety."

Paul Tillich, on the other hand, calls for a completely new understanding of love:

> A fresh interpretation of love is needed . . . an interpretation that shows that love is basically not an emotional but an ontological power, that it is the essence of life itself, namely the dynamic reunion of that which is separated.

Ontological love, love as the most basic process of being, a process that seeks to reunite, to hold together all that has been separated; what might such a conception of love have to say to our contemporary breakdown in communication?

In the first place it would insist that the purpose, the very essence of communication is to unite rather than to divide—an understanding with ramifications all the way from the White House and Congress to what happens in the Sunday coffee hour after church.

Suppose, for example, that when we talk, when we set out to communicate on this simplest of levels, we focus on the other person and not solely on ourselves. Suppose we consider the person with whom we speak not as adversary, customer, competitor, inquisitor, or judge but rather as a child of God; one who bears discoveries, disasters, experiences, even explanations that might be shared, communicated, looked at from many angles, and then incorporated into a wider, truer view of life.

Suppose we began to listen rather than just waiting our turn to speak. Ambrose Bierce defines a bore as "a person who talks when you wish him to listen." If we were to start listening, there's no telling what might happen, what we might learn!

Or again, what if we began to choose our words so as to help others comprehend; not to impress or confuse, overwhelm or persuade but first and foremost to promote understanding? Suppose we began to seek the *good* of those we speak to as a basic posture, a fundamental stance. Might that also be love in action? Could that provide the missing link, Paul's *sine qua non* that transforms an empty din into a dialogue?

A parable called "The Rabbi's Gift" might say it best. M. Scott Peck recounts the story in his book *The Different Drum*. A certain monastery had fallen on hard times. Cynicism, secularism, commercialism had taken a heavy toll, and the once thriving house had dwindled to an abbot and four elderly monks. In the woods nearby was a hut that the local rabbi used as a place of meditation, and one day the abbot paid him a visit.

As they talked, the abbot voiced his fear of the impending doom of his monastery. He asked for advice, but the rabbi could offer only sympathy; his synagogue faced similar problems. The two old men wept together. However, as the abbot was leaving, the rabbi bade him farewell with this curious comment: "The only thing I can tell you is that the Messiah is one of you."

As the holy man reentered the cloister, the monks crowded round, "What did the rabbi say?"

"Only one thing, and that was very cryptic. He said that the Messiah is one of us, whatever that means."

The old men pondered this: *The Messiah is one of us; how can this be? Who can it be? Perhaps he meant the abbot our leader, or Brother Thomas, who is certainly a holy man. But then Brother Eldred, for all his crotchety ways is usually right about things, maybe the rabbi meant him. Surely not Philip, he is so passive, a real nobody. But whenever you need him he is at your side, almost by magic. Of course the rabbi didn't mean me. That's impossible! Yet supposing he did? Oh God, not me.*

So they contemplated and the longer they contemplated, the more the monks began to treat one another, even themselves with new respect. After all, you never could be sure. Neighbors began to sense the new aura surrounding these men, radiating out to all they met. People began visiting the monastery to pray again. They brought along friends, and friends brought more friends. Some of the younger men lingered to discuss things with the monks, and before you knew it, one asked if he could join, then another and another. Within a few years that monastery was once again a place of learning and of light, thanks to the gift of one wise rabbi.

"The Messiah is one of you." What would happen, what could happen to our communication, to the whole intricate web of our relationships if we recognized the presence of the Messiah within each one of us? What could happen if the love that Christ embodied and lived out were to find its roots and its reality within our daily lives? Might we then, at last, begin to speak with the tongues of mortals and of angels?

——————— ✚ ———————

Take all our words, Lord God—our speaking, our silence too—and weave them through and through with the fabric of your love. Teach us to listen and to speak as in the presence of the Christ. Amen.

2

The Knowledge Deficit

━━━━━━━━━━━━━━━━━━━━━━━━━━━━━━━ ⊕

If I have prophetic powers, and understand all mysteries and all knowledge, . . . but do not have love, I gain nothing.

hristianity, throughout its history, has displayed a decided ambivalence toward this elemental human goal, the quest for knowledge. As far back as the second century A.D., Tertullian—himself a brilliant scholar—contended ferociously against any kind of philosophizing or scholarly debate concerning the faith. The Christian gospel, he argued, is simply and solely God's truth, once revealed, handed down by the apostles, given to us to be believed . . . period!

> A plague on Aristotle who taught . . . dialectic, the art which destroys as much as it builds. . . . For it reconsiders every point to make sure it never finishes a discussion. What has Jerusalem to do with Athens, the Church with the Academy, the Christian with the heretic?

So declaimed Tertullian. These fierce denunciations did not go unanswered. Other theologians, among them Origen of Alexandria and later Augustine, welcomed the powers of the intellect as divine gifts; gifts to be gratefully employed in the investigation and further elucidation of God's truth.

To this day some Christians would bar the door to knowledge or at least set narrow boundaries to its pursuit. Such fervent believers claim to present only the "simple Bible truths" and condemn all scholarly research as the wiles of Satan, out to lure believers into first questioning, then doubting, and finally forfeiting their faith.

Simplicity has its attractions, but we live within an enormously complex universe. The psalmist writes, "The Lord protects the simple." But penciled in the margin of my "working" Bible are the words: *True, but the stupid are another matter!*

Therefore let me begin by setting out a plea for the Christian intellect. It is the mark of a tiny and timorous faith to seek to stifle debate, to close off investigation, to seal off the mind from entire areas of research with regard to the scriptures and to God.

On my morning walk recently I noticed these telling words on the notice board of a neighboring church: *Christ died to save us from our sins, not from our minds.* And I wanted to shout, "Hallelujah!"—which would probably have gone unnoticed on the streets of Greenwich Village! The British theologian J. B. Phillips expressed much the same idea in the title of one of his books: *Your God Is Too Small.* And your God *is* too small if your faith demands that you fix blinders over your eyes for fear of what they might see.

After all, it was God who created this vast, intricate, and eternally fascinating universe; and then set within the human creation these inquisitive, probing minds with which to explore it. God devised the laws, principles, and constants, the seasons, systems—lack of systems too—that govern everything we know, everything we experience.

Instead of fencing in our view of God around a few well-worn, time-honored dogmas, we must engage in an ongoing expansion of the available definitions and descriptions in order to embrace the ever more magnificent creation that the mind is only beginning to comprehend.

The Jewish religion, from which Christianity draws both roots and rich heritage, has a world-renowned tradition of reverence for learning. Look, for example, at

~21~

Judaism's one and only religious title "rabbi," which means "teacher." Rabbi Abraham Heschel has written,

> The Greeks learned in order to comprehend. The Hebrews learned in order to revere. . . . It is wrong to define education as *preparation* for life. Learning *is* life, a supreme experience of living, a climax of existence. . . . True learning is a way of relating ourselves to something which is both eternal and universal.

Learning, wisdom, knowledge is a sacred gift, entrusted by the Creator; it is to be *used*, fully and strenuously used in God's service, to God's glory.

Having agreed upon all this, how is it that Paul—himself one of the most gifted thinkers of his day—can write such words as these to the church in Corinth: "Where is the one who is wise? Where is the scribe? Where is the debater of this age? Has not God made foolish the wisdom of this world?" (1 Corinthians 1:20).

And if I have prophetic powers, and understand all mysteries and all knowledge, . . . but do not have love, I gain nothing.

At this point, one thing should be made clear. In these opening verses, Paul is not putting down the various gifts he deals with. It is not his intent to say that communication, knowledge, faith, self-sacrifice are intrinsically worthless. Paul's point is that if persons receive and exercise these rich blessings of God *without love*, they become of no value whatsoever.

For Paul, knowledge *is* a great potential blessing. But he has learned in his own life how swiftly knowledge without love can turn from blessing to curse. Paul's expertise in the Law permitted him to stand by and hold the cloaks of those who stoned Stephen—the first Christian martyr—to death.

In our own day, the quest for knowledge without love—for knowledge as a tool, a weapon with which to seek advantage over others—has led to a school system, for example, of such inequality that many children are condemned the moment they step through that system's doors.

As for those who *are* educated, one has to ask what it is they are educated for. Chaplain Peter Gomes of Harvard has written, "The world is full of people who know more than is good for them and not enough that is good for all of us." Theologian Sallie McFague comments,

We need scarcely be reminded in a post-Auschwitz, post-Vietnam, post-Watergate society of the results of an education designed to produce people whose technical knowledge is impressive, but whose moral and emotional lives are desiccated.

Colleges and universities—the indictment runs—often

have simply been centers for teaching people how to outwit other people. If that seems extreme, think of how a college degree, especially a degree from one of the more prestigious institutions, admits one to a whole new world of contacts, customs, wit and wisdom, dress, decorum, language, and lineage; an elite world to which a majority of people never have a hope of gaining access.

So learning without love, as Paul saw long ago, is learning that sets people apart rather than drawing them together; is learning that divides into classes, clans, cliques rather than helping folk to understand, have compassion for, live at peace with one another. Such knowledge is worth nothing and less than nothing.

But learning based on love, knowledge that takes as its starting point, its fundamental axiom, God's love for all in Christ, and our answering, responding love for God and one another; such knowledge is, as the psalmist says, "too wonderful. It is high. I cannot attain it." Yet it is this unattainable wonder that Paul sets before us as both vision and goal.

To learn in order to serve, not merely to succeed. To seek, in all study and research to promote only the good of humankind, never the destruction of any part of it. To turn the vast and as yet virtually unchallenged resources of the brain away from the obsession with the marketplace, the production and promotion of violence, vanity, and greed;

and to focus the collective mental energies of a multitude of scholars, scientists, artists—ordinary citizens too—on seeking out new ways, truer ways to live together on this beautiful blue ball we have inherited for life . . . for life!

Imagine what it might mean, a new Manhattan Project with all the urgency, drama, and vitality of the 1940s; but this time focused, not on unleashing the powers of destruction, but on opening up the global reservoirs of goodwill, trust, hospitality, and hope all across this shadowed and imperiled globe.

Not long ago, as I was closeted away preparing a sermon, my study was interrupted by a surprise visit from an old friend. Larry—a genuine renaissance man with degrees from The Curtis Institute of Music, Temple, Yale, and the European Business School at Fontainbleau—had been organist for several years at a church I served as pastor. While in New York on business, he stopped to say hello. We wandered into the silent shadows of our historic sanctuary and, locating a key on the organ console, Larry turned the instrument on and played a magnificent fragment of Bach from memory.

As I stood and marveled, it dawned on me that what I was witnessing at work was knowledge based on love. All those years of study, practice, expertise, and interpretation combined, all the *knowledge* that went into producing that glorious cascade of indescribable sound, while beneath and around, above, and throughout the whole of it there was a love, a passion, a commitment to beauty and to sharing that beauty that transformed mere performance into sheer and unalloyed praise.

To harness knowledge to love is the secret to overcoming the knowledge deficit. The challenge is to re-evaluate our own uses, our stewardship of these resources of wisdom, learning, and experience we have been granted; to view them with freshly opened eyes as gifts, given for the benefit of all God's peoples, not for private profit alone. We are called today to seek out ways to promote the cause of understanding, with all the rich and varied meanings of that word, across the family of humankind. To do this is finally to begin to probe the deepest secret of this universe, to explore what Paul has called "the breadth and length and height and depth, and to know the love of Christ that surpasses knowledge." It is of such a love that Paul has written,

> *If I have prophetic powers, and understand all mysteries and all knowledge, . . . but do not have love, I am nothing.*

———— ✢ ————

Teach us, good Lord, to share unbegrudgingly the gifts of knowledge entrusted to us without concern for personal gain. Let us share the gifts of knowledge freely, openly, generously, lovingly. Then surprise us with the knowledge, the newer, fuller wisdom we will receive in return. Through Christ who is your Wisdom, your Word of love made flesh for us. Amen.

3

You Gotta Believe

☩

*And if I have all faith, so as to remove mountains,
but do not have love, I am nothing.*

ome months ago I attended one of those
luncheons to which religious leaders of all
stripes and varieties get invited and at which
we were to hear an address by a leading ecu-
menical churchman. The luncheon was reasonable—your
customary hotel chicken; the company, stimulating, including many distinguished members of the clergy—I
was seated with two former Presidents of the World
Council of Churches! And the speech was genuinely in-
spiring, which is not always the case. But it was the response to that speech that got me thinking.

The speaker had focused on the twin concerns of poverty and peace, challenging us, from our varied religious backgrounds, to a common effort in these closely linked areas. He sat down amid a respectful hush, and the chair invited questions from the floor.

Immediately a young man, leaning against the door jamb at the rear and with a strangely amicable grin on his face, launched into a tirade. He accused the speaker and by implication the audience of being traitors to the faith and smilingly consigned us to hell because we had tampered with the word of God as contained fully and finally in the King James' Version and were consorting with socialists, Communists, and other such emissaries of Satan.

The speaker—praises be!—had the grace to answer his assailant in a gentle, positive way and the incident soon passed. But as I read over Paul's words here about "faith, so as to remove mountains," my thoughts returned to that smilingly angry young man.

As I recall, my initial reaction was to say, "What a fool!" and to feel anger at his disrespect for our speaker, at the young man's ignorance in parading all that half-baked nonsense before such a distinguished group. But I moved swiftly from "What a fool!" to "What a pity!" How sad that someone could be so foolishly misled. Only later, after much reflection, could I add two further reactions.

The first was, "What courage!" What courage to

face a roomful of strangers with such a provocative and hostile message. And then finally it dawned on me, "What faith!" What faith that young heckler must have had to say what he did in that setting. He must have believed truly and deeply.

What is faith? What is the shape and substance, the inner dynamics, the psychological and emotional ingredients that make up this dimension of existence we call faith? Let me admit at the outset that this topic is far too complex to treat in one small chapter of one small book; just as one slim volume of fourteen chapters and a preface is, by no means, a complete or even adequate treatment of the subject of love. What I can attempt to do, however, is to make a few introductory comments.

In the first place, whatever faith is, it is undeniably powerful. Not too long ago, popular opinion scoffed at faith as being merely the capacity to believe things, all sorts of weird and wonderful things. It was that brilliantly savage skeptic Ambrose Bierce who composed the following definition for his *Devil's Dictionary*: "Faith, n. Belief without evidence in what is told by one who speaks without knowledge, of things without parallel."

H. L. Mencken once wrote, "Faith may be defined briefly as an illogical belief in the occurrence of the improbable." Thus the secular world came to confuse faith with credulity, the ability to swallow entire litanies of obligatory teachings—no matter how far-fetched—without batting an eyelid or crossing a finger. Alice holds a memorable conversation with the Queen in Lewis Carroll's *Through the Looking Glass*. She asserts, "One *can't* believe impossible things." The Queen replies, "I dare say you haven't had much practice. When I was your age, I always did it for half-an-hour a day. Why, sometimes I've believed as many as six impossible things before breakfast."

But faith is more than gullibility. Look, for example, at the new appreciation within medical science for what used to be called "faith healing" but nowadays is known as psychosomatic medicine. We are witnessing today a new appreciation of the role of belief, the realization that a patient must not only understand but also place confidence, trust, and vitally committed hope in the processes of recovery. Faith *can* work wonders, and the medical community is beginning to discover this again.

Or consider the awesome potential of human faith in leaders and causes: the way a Roosevelt, Churchill, Hitler, Mussolini, a Khomeini even, or Saddam Hussein can inspire whole nations to great heights, as well as to abysmal depths. Most recent elections in this nation too have been billed as an act of faith. Whom do you trust; which candidate can you really believe? This faith *is* a powerful thing.

Faith is also a paradoxical thing. It can turn disease

into health; yet through voodoo, hypnotic suggestion, and the like, it can also turn health into disease. Faith can mobilize throngs into armies for justice or into mobs bent on violence and death. Faith can transform fools into millionaires and millionaires into fools again.

Even when the discussion is limited to faith in God, one still confronts paradox. Fervent faith in God aroused and empowered the Crusades and the resulting slaughter of hosts of innocent Jews and Muslims, not to mention the Christians who also perished. It was faith in God that launched the Inquisition, equipped torture chambers, and kindled fires that burned heretics all across the Middle Ages. Faith in God right now, misguided as it may be, is whipping up the volatile emotions of marginal individuals who go on to commit murder or carry out hate crimes against Jews, homosexuals, minority group members—persons whose only fault is being different.

Faith in God has fragmented the Christian community into innumerable faith-filled yet fiercely hostile camps. Indeed, when the roll *is* called up yonder this division may be recognized as the greatest sin, our most disastrous failure. We have been so zealous to defend to the death our own exclusive concept of faith that we have ignored the one thing really necessary; the one thing even Paul, that great teacher and preacher of *faith* was forced to admit took precedence. We have forgotten love. For faith, as Paul said, may be able to move mountains, but only love can move the human heart.

What is faith's purpose, when all is said and done? Is it not a way, *the* way back into the heart of God, as we find ourselves set right through trust in Christ? But who, then, is this God? What is this God's will for us, if and when we do have faith?

> Beloved let us love one another, because love is from God; everyone who loves is born of God and knows God. Whoever does not love does not know God, for God is love.
>
> —1 John 4:7-8

These words were penned to Christians long ago, Christians who were strong in faith yet had not learned how to love. Again we read,

> For this is the message you have heard from the beginning, that we should love one another. . . . How does God's love abide in anyone who has the world's goods and sees a brother or sister in need and yet refuses to help?
>
> —1 John 3:11, 17

So faith is noble, faith is powerful; it is essential. But faith is ultimately the means to an end. And that end is God. And that God is love. Consequently faith that does not serve that end—faith that results in intolerance, condemnation, even violence; faith that produces lovelessness toward the poor and unfortunate; faith that is used to support legalized injustice or in any way sets barriers between God's children; all this is bad faith, failed faith, poisoned and perverted faith. And as Paul has put it, such faith is rubbish, worth nothing at all.

Last spring, surfing the late-night channels, I came across that movie classic *Chariots of Fire*. I thrilled again to its pounding music, its breathtaking photography, its vibrant action. It was a film about faith, a stirring presentation of the dedication of two exemplary young men to their individual beliefs.

But at the end I realized something was missing. Only one brief line across the screen recorded the truest triumph of one of those young heroes Eric Liddell. It read as follows: "Eric Liddell—missionary, died in Occupied China at the end of World War II." But that was where the love came in, right where the movie ended. That was where the goal was finally gained, grasped, and held, at least for Liddell. And without that, this presentation, for all its splendor, was sadly incomplete.

Some years ago in Scotland, I bought and read the official biography of Eric Liddell—a book that recounts the rest of the story, that goes on from the 1924 Olympics, what the world saw as his finest hour. It tells of twenty years beyond; twenty years in China, twenty years of quiet unspectacular preaching, teaching, doing youth work with the children he always loved best, coaching, praying, hoping, struggling, and finally dying, separated from his young wife and child, worn out from helping others, in a Japanese Internment Camp in 1945.

The chapter that tells of Eric's death is called "The Breaking of the Tape." It describes how Liddell—having kept the faith, and then having gone beyond faith to live the love of Christ—crossed that far-off finish line in triumph. Not this time in Paris's Colombes Stadium, before a cheering Olympic throng but before a far greater host, that cloud of witnesses described in Hebrews, the communion of all saints. For Eric Liddell, life went beyond faith and found itself and spent itself in love.

So let faith be strong. Let us hold firm our commitment to Christ as Savior and Lord, but let us be even more careful that our faith bears fruit in love. For Paul has written,

And if I have all faith, so as to remove mountains, but do not have love, I am nothing.

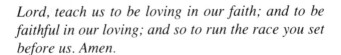

Lord, teach us to be loving in our faith; and to be faithful in our loving; and so to run the race you set before us. Amen.

4

The Right Thing for the Wrong Reason

⊕

If I give away all I have, and if I deliver my body to be burned, but have not love, I gain nothing.

hat a positively outrageous, perhaps even radical, certainly uncomfortable piece of scripture this thirteenth chapter of First Corinthians is turning out to be! One might have been excused for thinking one was launching out on something altogether lovely; a sublime series of gentle musings clustered around that delightful theme, love-sweet-love. But already Paul has attacked his readers on at least four fronts. He has called into question our miraculous modern means of communication. He has challenged the value of our knowledge, science, education. He has cast doubt upon the integrity of faith, even "faith that moves mountains." And now, of all things, he is assaulting charitable giving.

If I give away everything I possess, and even if I sacrifice my very life for the cause, but do not do it all out of love, I gain nothing (author's paraphrase).

What kind of talk is that for the church of today, a church that depends for its very existence—so it seems—on the regular, dependable, ever-increasing generosity of its members? What kind of talk is that for folk who agonize during every fall stewardship season, debating whether they can afford an increase in their giving?

Now hold everything. Don't fly off the handle, or worse yet, call up your church, demand your pledge card, and feed it to the office shredder. Paul is not really attacking giving *per se*. But Paul *is* raising that old, and for him, all-important question of motivation. Just as with faith, knowledge, and the rest, these gifts of God, he suggests, are not evil in and of themselves. On the contrary, they are potentially the source of great blessing and true joy. However, this will be the result if, and only if, these gifts are motivated by a basic concern for the welfare of others.

The question of motivation; that thorny old dilemma that faces Thomas à Becket in T. S. Eliot's *Murder in the*

Cathedral when, just as he is about to be cut down at the high altar of Canterbury by King Henry's four "rebel" knights, the Archbishop wrestles with whether he is actually seeking death, pursuing martyrdom. He concludes,

> The last temptation is the greatest treason:
> to do the right deed for the wrong reason.

Why *do* people give to Christ's church or to anything else for that matter? What motivations lurk beneath those scraps of paper in the collection baskets and pledge envelopes? In my own experience I must consider many motivations; a complex, conflicting host of rationales.

People can give out of guilt; seeking to make up for some previous offense, to atone for foolish, thoughtless, even dishonest or violent actions in the past. Yet the very heart of the gospel, those words of assurance proclaimed in churches Sunday after Sunday, cry out that all has *been* forgiven, that in Christ all guilt is washed away. There is no need to purchase God's forgiveness, even if such a thing were possible, because that purchase has been made already. We *are* redeemed in Christ. So if you are giving out of guilt, don't take back your gift, but let Paul help you find a better reason, a richer, fuller motivation.

Still others, or a part within each and every person, give from a sense of obligation. It's something one owes in return for all that God has given. Yet once again the Gospels assert—even if common sense did not—that if one gives in order to repay, one might as well quit immediately. We owe everything we are, have, and hope for to the Lord; any conceivable offering in return must seem a petty insult, a childish gesture over against that vast and universal indebtedness.

The motivation of pride spurs some people on. There is a clear satisfaction to be found in giving, so long as others somehow can be informed. All those names carved in gold across white marble in the museums and galleries; inscribed toward the rear of concert programs—donors, patrons, partners—there is an undeniable thrill in the role of public benefactor.

Even when only the recipient knows, there is still a wondrous glow to be discovered around the doling out of charity to someone clearly less gifted, less able, less successful. Jesus had one thing to say about such givers: "They already have their reward."

Some give from fear, trusting that the occasional judicious application of a modicum of charity can keep the poor from turning ugly. One of the great nineteenth-century reforming preachers once remarked, "In the war between the haves and the have-nots, many will give lavishly to avoid the day of reckoning." It's cheaper in the short run to buy Band-Aids than to pay for major surgery—especially when that surgery means complete social reformation.

Allied to these are all who give out of calculation. It helps reduce the tax bill. I love the tale of the forthright (if rather foolhardy) pastor who announced the offering thus: "Now let us return to the Lord according to that which we reported on Form 1040, line 23."

There are those who give in response to peer pressure, as with such programs as United Way: "Everyone else in the office has given." There are those who give out of family tradition: "Our family has always supported the church." There are even those who try to build what more cynical clergy call "fire escapes"—large, late-in-life donations to erect structures for protection of the donor from the heat in the hereafter.

A whole raft, a vast smorgasbord of reasons, rationales, motivations for giving. And one thing should be emphasized: whatever the motivation, the gift still can be used for good; even the grimiest, most tattered and bloodstained dollar bills can buy food for the hungry. But unless that gift is given out of love and the motivation is to bless another, not oneself, then the blessing will be all one way. Nothing, zero, zilch, will reflect back upon the giver.

Where does this leave all of us who do give? Deflated, if not demoralized; feeling that having made a reasonably generous gift, that donation has been unfairly questioned, the gift horse has had every one of its molars carefully examined? But that's not the point! What Paul has in mind is not to put *down* giving but to lift it *up*, to elevate it to new and higher level. Paul says to all who give, all who sacrifice to support the mission of our Lord, whether through the church or whatever: "Yes my friend! Do it! Keep on giving. Give even more if possible. But please don't miss the boat. For God's sake, for *your own* sake, don't miss the boat."

All gifts to God can bring about good. But gifts given out of love bear a double blessing. Just like "The quality of mercy" in Portia's speech from *The Merchant of Venice*: "It blesseth him that gives, and him that takes." Gifts motivated by love bless both giver and receiver.

Remember this every time you write a check to the church, drop an envelope in the plate, send a donation through the mail. Do not, please do not miss the boat. Please do not ever give grimly, grudgingly, or through gritted teeth. If you are going to give, why not enjoy it? Remember those other words of Paul: "God loves a cheerful giver."

Some months ago I rushed over the river to Brooklyn, after my own church service, to attend a 1:30 P.M. service at Gethsemane Church—a Presbyterian congregation for prisoners, exprisoners, and their families supported by my congregation's mission dollars. Wasn't that a bit much, (one might ask), two services back to back? Didn't I run the risk of an overdose?

Yet the spirit that I met, that met me at the door; the privilege of sitting in rickety pews and seeking God with fellow Christians from all kinds of backgrounds and life stories, the sheer panic and then wonder of being asked to write a letter—over coffee and sandwiches after church—to a fellow Presbyterian in jail, and in all this the thrill of seeing my own church's gifts at work, the life that God has channeled through our modest sacrifices; and then to become part of it, welcomed to its heart, that was a joy I cherish, yes, covet for every believer at least once in a while.

Could it be we get so little joy from giving because we hardly ever see the end results? Might it be true that if we were to follow up our gifts with our lives, to spend an hour or two in personal involvement: serving food at a hostel for people with AIDS, spending a night on the staff of a homeless shelter—then straw would turn to gold; checks would turn to living, breathing lives; and all those graphs, pie charts, and percentages from the stewardship campaign would be transformed into amazing grace? Love is never all that easy, but it is still a whole lot simpler to love a child of God than a check you drop into the mail.

To give out of love. To see a need and meet it, not because we ought to, but because we want to. To respond to another's hurt or hunger not out of guilt, but as one child of God to another. To sense in all our giving at least an echo of the joy we feel Christmas morning as our loved ones unwrap the gifts we have lovingly selected.

Imagine the glow that Samaritan felt riding away from the inn the next morning, leaving the wounded traveler bedded down and provided for. Picture the bliss of that woman as she anointed Jesus' feet with fragrant ointment, then knelt beside her Lord in quiet peace. Then glimpse the joy our Lord must have felt, still must feel, each time you and I accept his gift of life eternal and act upon it. That same joy can be ours if we can only move our giving out of duty, fear, and calculating worry into love. For Paul has written,

If I give away all I have, and if I deliver my body to be burned, but have not love, I gain nothing.

———— ✚ ————

Lord, unlock our worried minds, unseal our frightened hearts, unfreeze our frigid lives, and help us to know the joy that awaits us within the gifts we have already given. Then teach us to grow in joy, in giving, and in love. Through Christ, himself the giver and the gift. Amen.

5

A Cup O' Kindness Yet

Love is patient; love is kind.

e may read this immortal thirteenth chapter of First Corinthians in two ways. The first treats the piece in isolation, complete in and of itself—a glorious hymn to love—one of the most lyrical and, at the same time, profound of meditations. And this approach is not entirely without merit; the chapter *is* sublime.

Yet one of the most far-reaching conclusions of biblical scholarship is the realization that in this vast book, the Bible, we do not simply have a collection of unrelated teachings, an enormous anthology of advice and counsel about life into which one may dip at random and come up with something helpful. Rather we have here a story, an ages-long narrative, written in many forms and voices, at many times and places, written from the viewpoint of many philosophies and perspectives; but a story nonetheless, with a beginning, a development, a climax, and at least a provisional conclusion. Despite its seeming contradictions and contrasting points of view, this story is one story. It is the story of God's love: God's creating, dreaming, yearning, and then suffering and redeeming love.

Therefore to lift one chapter out of this story and study it in isolation—while seemingly helpful and productive—is finally the wrong approach and ultimately self-defeating. Each text, each chapter, each verse must be read in context, in relationship to and in conversation with other passages and points of view in order for its fullest meaning to be grasped.

So it is with this chapter we are studying. Far from being an isolated fragment of immortal poetry, 1 Corinthians 13 is one stage of a long, complex, and most specific debate. It is part of a letter written to a church in trouble; a letter written by a man who, through his preaching of the gospel, had founded that church; a man whose heart is being torn apart as he sees this church in which he has invested so much of himself—his own faith, hope, and love—in such a desperate plight.

The problem of the Corinthian church was, in a word, *factions*: rival parties, contending schools of thought, competing cliques and groupings. In the earlier chapters Paul has spelled out in practical terms some possible solutions, some approaches to settling their disputes. In this thirteenth chapter, however, Paul seeks higher ground. He wants to get above, or better yet, below these quarrels, issues, antipathies. He wants to lay the groundwork, a new and stronger foundation for a new and stronger church.

When Paul points out that one may have the gifts of eloquence, all the communication skills in the world, but without love these are only an empty din, he has actual and specific individuals in mind. He can picture particular leaders of that troubled church who spoke in tongues, who had powerfully persuasive eloquence, but who used these gifts not to unite but to divide. When he writes of having wisdom and understanding, faith so as to move mountains, Paul knows precisely to whom he is writing—individuals who have used their learning and faith not to build up but to tear down the community. When he speaks of giving everything away, even sacrificing life itself—these are not mere noble aspirations—he speaks directly to persons who have sought to dominate this church by their own capacity to give far beyond the ability of the average believer.

The situation is no different with the text for this chapter. It is not exactly a startling revelation to say, "Love is patient; love is kind." That's hardly a fresh insight into the dynamics of love. On the contrary, it's almost a cliché, one of those texts embroidered onto cushions, doilies, and samplers, set out in hearts and roses on a Valentine's card or frilly bookmark. But Paul writes these words to a congregation whose members have been anything *but* patient, who seem to have forgotten that such a thing as kindness exists. Indeed they are at one another's throats, denouncing and condemning one another, squabbling even as they sit around the table of the Lord. And when Paul says to Christians like these "Love is patient; love is kind," he is preaching the entire gospel to them; the gospel that both judges and delivers out of judgment.

The Greek word used here for patience means specifically the kind of patience that relates to people rather than to natural circumstances, disease, disaster, and the like. It carries with it a suggestion of suffering, as brought out in the King James Version: "Love suffereth long." This particular kind of patience implies "putting up with," enduring, even accepting injury from someone, without the need to pay back or retaliate. The use of this specific word suggests that Christians who seek love must be prepared to know some pain; to live some sorrow; to accept the other person in, through, and despite much hurt and deep frustration.

Much of what we read, hear, and view today describes quite the opposite: a painless love, ever blissful; replete with laughter, fun, multiple and uncomplicated sexual satisfactions; a love that wanders hand-in-hand through blossoming fields of everlasting springtime. But the love whose story runs like a golden thread from Genesis to Revelation is far different. It is a love that "bears our griefs and carries our sorrows"; a love which, as the prophet Isaiah saw it, was like a tender lamb led to the slaughter, which does not open its mouth in protest or in anger; yet in so doing heals, redeems, and unifies.

This is a love that believes it is better to undergo violence than to inflict it. How unfashionable, how utterly reactionary! In this era of universal litigation and victims' rights, this time when everybody wants to blame and sue everybody else for everything conceivable, how utterly passé to say, "Love suffereth long . . . is kind."

I am reminded of that rich word *atonement*, or at-*one*-ment, which signifies the act of breaking down the walls of separation, aggravation, litigation, of every kind of human alienation whatsoever, and of bringing folk together through love, this *other* love—this love Paul sings of, which is both patient and kind.

Please do not misunderstand. I am not proposing that a battered wife, an abused youngster, an exploited employee, an oppressed minority should accept his or her lot and suffer patiently and silently. That is not the way of love. Ambrose Bierce once defined that kind of patience as "a minor form of despair, disguised as a virtue." Such unjust situations cry out to be amended. But even such amendment should not be undertaken in anger or vengeful counterviolence; rather with all the skill, intelligence, strength, and patience too that genuine love can muster.

In a time when many perceive a crisis in leadership—a leadership gap between what people yearn for and what is currently available—an old leader comes to mind; one who lived, walked, and died to show this nation and the world the patient, nonviolent path to reconciling love. Thirty years ago the Reverend Doctor Martin Luther King, Jr., wrote these words about violence and love:

> The ultimate weakness of violence is that it is a descending spiral, begetting the very thing it seeks to destroy. Instead of diminishing evil, it multiplies it. . . . Through violence you may murder the liar, but you cannot murder the lie nor establish the truth. Through violence you may murder the hater, but you do not murder hate. In fact violence merely increases hate. So it goes. Returning violence for violence multiplies violence, adding deeper darkness to a night already devoid of stars. Darkness cannot drive out darkness: only light can do that. Hate cannot drive out hate: only love can do that.

As for kindness, I'm afraid the church has never been that good at being kind. William Barclay, that wise and perceptive old Scot, writes, "So much Christianity is good but unkind." He goes on to tell of indubitably good and holy men who instituted and led the Inquisition and similar atrocities. Barclay asserts, "So many *good* church people would have sided with the rulers not with Jesus if they had had to deal with the woman taken in adultery."

"The milk of human kindness," Shakespeare called it. What a lovely yet rare gift—to alleviate some of the misery; to improve at least a fraction of the lot of those around; to ease some pain, soothe some fears, tend hurts, dispel at least a little of the loneliness and neglect that cross your daily path. "To lend each other a hand when we're falling," says Saint Brendan, in Frederick Buechner's novel of his life, "perhaps that's the only work that matters in the end."

A modest aim for life, this aim of kindness. Yet one which might move this world a little, if not transform it. An aim that might leave it better than we found it; lend a little meaning, a little value, substance, vision to these barren, self- and sensation-seeking days.

Those quite unlivable, yet also quite unforgettable words of the Master: "Love your enemies, do good to those who hate you, bless those who curse you, pray for those who abuse you." I guess he never had to live in New York City or central Illinois or Mississippi or California either.

Or might the way of love still be the answer, the only method never really tried; the one hope left for a world that seems to be sliding back, bewitched by fear, prejudice, and ignorance, down that slope toward the dark with its grim store of unspeakable atrocities.

The way of love; the way of patience; the way of kindness, simple kindness in a relationship, a family, a community, a church, and a world. "We'll tak a cup o' kindness yet for auld lang syne," sang Robert Burns in a warm and welcoming song that has been called the national anthem of the human race. Yet will we? Will we ever try it—sip that cup, live that patient and kind love? Or will we merely read this passage for its beauty, its elevated thought, its matchless poetry; and then return to walk the ancient, twisted ways of resentment, anger, hatred, fear, and dusty death?

———— ✢ ————

Lord, we cannot do it on our own. We have tried and failed before. So root your love within us, that by your grace, we might begin, right where we are, to build at least one corner of the kingdom; one place, one human community where patience and the milk of human kindness can still flow and spread and even yet redeem. Amen.

6

The Green-Ey'd Monster

_____ ✚

Love is not jealous (RSV).

For as long as there is jealousy and quarreling among you, are you not of the flesh, and behaving according to human inclinations?

—1 Corinthians 3:3

n his tiny jewel of a book *The Greatest Thing in the World,* Henry Drummond suggests that in these opening verses Paul has taken the radiant light of love and directed its beam through a prism, "the magnificent prism of his inspired intellect" so that now we see love displayed according to its elements, its interlocking and compensatory parts. This chapter will continue to focus upon this radiant spectrum, looking at four words from the fourth verse: *Love is not jealous* (RSV).

Envy seems an elusive emotion for many in this day and age. It's as if we don't think of ourselves as envious or jealous anymore. Ask people when they last experienced the pangs of classic envy, and they might be hard-pressed to come up with an instance. Or if they do, it will hardly seem all that serious. But before abandoning the topic, perhaps we ought to take time to dig a little deeper.

A specific setting comes to mind. I am seated on a lounge chair on the grassy bluff in front of our island log cabin in Maine, overlooking one little corner of Casco Bay. It is a sunny, breezy Saturday morning—say in early August—and there, before and below me, cruising effortlessly out toward the open ocean from the moorings of the Portland Yacht Club, is a spectacular armada. Vessels of all shapes, sizes, and configurations glide across the Bay. They have one thing in common: every one of them is far bigger, far grander, far more glossy than my own somewhat battered, thirteen-year-old boat moored round the point at the island boatyard. As I watch, an emotion that just might be described as envy nibbles round the edges of my psyche.

Of course, that's only one scenario. I suspect that most of us who dwell in the affluent West in this late twentiethth century could contribute an experience at least as real, at least as wrenchingly frustrating. And it's not only envy over material possessions that gives rise to such emotion. Someone else gets a job, a promotion, a wife or husband, an award or *re*ward you felt you deserved, and you rediscover envy. (I've never quite forgiven the Royal Air Force for promoting an obvious "yes-man" to the illustrious rank of corporal, when I had earned the highest examination marks in all of Bomber Command!)

This book the Bible knows about envy. Look again at the Ten Commandments, where number ten—that one concerning coveting—is far more detailed and comprehensive than any of the rest, except perhaps the one about the Sabbath. Indeed, the first crime recorded in scripture, after Adam and Eve's expulsion from Eden, is the fruit of envy; as Cain is so devoured by its blinding power that he slays his own brother because Abel's sacrifice was deemed acceptable and Cain's was not.

The root word for envy in the Greek that Paul uses is one that means "to boil." And that is precisely what happened within Cain; he boiled inside until all that pent-up emotion splashed over into deception, treachery, violence, and death.

According to Thomas Aquinas, the giant of medieval philosophy, "Envy is sadness at another person's good." Despite the accuracy of that observation, it is not forceful enough. Envy goes further. It moves from "sadness at another's good" to despising that other because of his or her good; and finally to happiness, rejoicing, if and when mischance befalls that other, even in the midst of good.

Such envy has its own perverted logic, its convoluted, whining dialogues that begin in childhood with "Why should *she* be allowed to do it?" or "How come *he* got one of those?" Finally it matures—if one can call it that—to the advanced level of "Oh, he's a wonderful person; and I don't grudge him his success, goodness knows he's done more than enough to get there. But did you know . . . ? I mean, I hate to have to tell you this, but . . . "

It sounds so familiar. We've heard it all before, said at least some of it too many times before.

One other observation about envy: it is a *kamikaze* kind of emotion, a suicidal act of self-indulgence. Gore Vidal confessed with characteristic candor and wit, "Whenever a friend succeeds, a little something in me dies." Joseph P. Kennedy—one who surely lived the pain of possessing almost everything yet failed to find peace—is reported to have commented, "More men die of jealousy than of cancer." Just like smoking or overeating, we know it's bad for us, that it may kill us in the end. Yet we cannot give it up.

Shakespeare referred to envy in *Othello* as "the green ey'd monster which doth mock the meat it feeds on." And that word *mock*, in Elizabethan English, means "to rot, decay, corrupt." Chrysostom, the silver-tongued preacher of fourth-century Constantinople, has written, "As a moth gnaws a garment, so doth envy consume a [person]." Dante's description of the penitents on the terrace of the envious in Hell includes the telling detail that their eyes are sewn up with wire. This indicates envy's most crippling result: it blinds so that one can no longer recognize reality.

Giotto depicts Envy as a creature with long ears to capture gossip and a serpent's tongue to poison reputations. Those who examine the picture may notice a further refinement: the tongue curves back to strike the eyes; again suggesting that jealousy blinds; recoils upon the bearer; fills that person's life with shadows, phantoms, passing fancies, and delusions. Such a person is forever reaching after something new, forever grasping after someone else's something new, never knowing true peace.

Yet for all this, for all the warnings of scholars and artists, all the teachings of the Bible, jealousy cannot be rooted out. Our modern way of life, our enormously "successful" consumer economy, may be seen as founded upon envy's fatal allure. "Envy is the gasoline on which a competitive society runs" according to critic John Lahr of *The New Yorker*.

Today's marketing and advertising seems to be based increasingly, not on a product's intrinsic merits but blatantly on envy: "Just look what so and so has got. . . . See what absolutely everyone is getting, wearing, driving. Why don't you have one too?" This "competitive consumption," this matter of keeping up with—even a little ahead of—the Joneses, appears to lie uncomfortably close to the mainspring, the driving mechanism of our global economy. Could we not consider the entire process to be one colossal exercise in envy?

Saint Paul saw envy at its worst. This fledgling church in Corinth, which he had founded and left in the hands of folk he thought to be responsible leaders, was being torn apart by an insidious combination of jealousy and pride. People had been coming to the *agape*—the love feast on the Sabbath—bringing picnic baskets of expensive foods and wines and keeping them to themselves, refusing to share with less affluent members. Is it any wonder that jealousy and hate was tearing this congregation apart? Is it any wonder that Paul writes in 1 Corinthians 3:3, "For as long as there is jealousy and quarreling among you, are you not of the flesh, and behaving according to human inclinations?"

These Corinthians had discovered, as everyone does sooner or later, that this world is far from egalitarian in its distribution of gifts. We may all be equal in *God's* sight, but in other matters such as fortune, health, appearance, and mental ability we are clearly unequally blessed.

Paul feels that two responses are possible. One response is that of pride on the part of the "haves" and virulent envy from the "have-nots." It is this response that the Corinthian church and most of us have followed much of the time since then. But Paul holds out another way—the way of love, the way of giving thanks for all God's gifts, no matter who possesses them; the way of offering thanks above all for the greatest gift of all, freely given to all, the gift of life made new in Christ.

With this gift, this daily gift of grace held firm, all other gifts are secondary. We can learn to experience true richness, a radically new wealth that results not from pride in how much we possess but from the realization of how little we truly need; not from any sense of superiority but from the vision of our common humanity. Then as Paul puts it in Romans, the Christian can "rejoice with those who rejoice, weep with those who weep" (12:15). Or as Paul also expresses it, the believer can "be all things to all people, if only we can win a few for life in Christ."

Only love offers a workable answer to the corrosion and corruption of a life deformed by jealousy, frustration, and dissatisfaction. Through trust in God, we can begin to share the gifts we have been given and live this love that neutralizes, that cancels out the poison of envy.

And finally in all this, we can discover peace; the peace that comes to those who find life, not in the pursuit of a multiplicity of things but in a singleness of purpose, in the simplicity of love.

Love is not envious.

So may we be.

———— ✦ ————

Lord, let your soothing, healing, cleansing Spirit wash across our bruised and battered lives. Take away all that festers and spoils within—all envy, discontent, all malice, every jealous thought. And teach us the true meaning of contentment based in love. Reveal to us the way to peace, that peace that passes understanding. Amen.

7

The Perils of Humility

———————————————————————————— ⊕

Love is not . . . boastful or arrogant or rude.

Or as the elegant King James Version puts it:

Charity vaunteth not itself, is not puffed up.

 hat master of the English language, Winston Churchill, when asked his opinion of his principal opponent in the House of Commons, Labour Party leader Clement Attlee, is said to have responded, "He is a modest little man who has a great deal to be modest about." Golda Meir's reputed comment matched that of Churchill when she retorted to one of her colleagues: "Don't be so humble. You're not that great!"

In our continuing examination of what I described in

the previous chapter as "the spectrum of love"—that range of qualities and attributes compiled by Saint Paul in 1 Corinthians 13, we turn now to examine this virtue called humility; we raise the question of what it means to be humble. How does one distinguish the genuine article from the false humility that is all too common, especially in religious circles. What does it mean, what might it mean in this world we live in nowadays to be humble?

Dame Edith Sitwell, the eccentric English poet (are there any other kind?) once claimed, "I have often wished I had time to cultivate modesty. . . . But I am too busy thinking about myself." The problem today seems to be not so much one of distinguishing true from false humility, as of discovering humility in *any* variety whatsoever.

There was a time—within living memory—when public personages, athletes, politicians, and the like, were expected to be modestly disarming in the spotlight; to attempt to back away from public acclaim; to confess, in that time-honored phrase: "Shucks! It was nothing, really." That myth lies in the dust. Hand anyone a microphone, direct a minicam or tape recorder in his or her direction, and it's "I'm the greatest!" or "We're number one!"

What happened to all those generations of teaching and tradition about modesty, self-effacement, the vulgarity of self-promotion, of pushing oneself forward?

Charity vaunteth not itself, is not puffed up.

Of course it always *was* this way in the entertainment business. In the old circus and snake-oil circuit, modesty was never in great demand. Perhaps this is where the explanation lies. Today everything is entertainment, from athletics to politics, from business to religion; the circus barker and the street hustler with their "Ladies and gentlemen, it is my amazing privilege to present to you the greatest, the most incredible, the one and only . . . " are the characteristic voices of our era.

But as for love: "love is not . . . boastful or arrogant or rude." What does Paul mean? What can we learn from him about humility in these most unhumble times?

In the first place, true humility requires an accurate assessment of the self. And it may be at this point that humility lost its acceptance, its credibility; because rather than an accurate assessment, humility came to mean a putting down, a *de*valuing, even a rejec-tion of the self.

William Penn in his "Fruits of Solitude" wrote, "No more lessen or dissemble thy merit, than overrate it; for though humility be a virtue, an affected one is not." A genuine, unaffected humility is no groveling, artificial self-despising that, when examined closely, is simply another inverse form of pride. True humility is a way of seeing ourselves as God sees us; a state of acceptance, of being at ease with what and who we are. As a reassuring elder once told me: "Don't worry about what other people are thinking about you. They probably aren't!"

That Roman centurion in the Gospel narrative, who came to Jesus seeking healing for his servant, knew his own importance: "For I also am a man set under authority, with soldiers under me; and I say to one, 'Go,' and he goes, and to another, 'Come,' and he comes, and to my slave, 'Do this,' and the slave does it" (Luke 7:8).

No false modesty there; simply a sane, accurate assessment of where he stood in the chain of command. That same assessment, however, led that honest, hardheaded military man to say to Jesus: "Lord, . . . I am not worthy to have you come under my roof."

One can't help wondering whether all the pseudo-humility of the past, that false tradition of wallowing in one's own unworthiness, might have prepared the way for today's more honest attitudes, including all the aggressive and abrasive self-endorsement and self-promotion that seem so prevalent.

Second, and equally important, true humility, humility that springs from the love of God working within, requires also an accurate assessment of the neighbor, of "the other." And here things become more difficult. An accurate assessment of the self is hard enough, but an accurate assessment of the neighbor—with all of the unknowns involved—seems impossible.

Yet that's what Jesus seemed to talk about much of the time: the elder brother of the prodigal; that unforgiving

servant whose own debt is canceled but who cannot forgive what's owed him; those griping vineyard workers,
angry because they were paid no more than the latecom-
ers; the Pharisee's sneering at his fellow-worshiper, the
publican; the Samaritan and those who passed by on the
other side. In these and a host of other parables, Jesus
presented a radical reassessment of the neighbor.

Jesus summarized this reassessment by teaching:
"You shall love your neighbor as yourself" (Mark 12:31).
Not *more* than yourself. Remember, I first called for "an
accurate assessment of your *own* self." Love your neighbor *as* yourself. And if we could all do that—no more, but
no less—then the homelessness and crime that plague our
cities; the racism, mob violence, and bigotry that tear
apart our world; the stark famine and warfare that turn
our evening news into one long elegy for the human race,
would be forever banished.

An accurate assessment of oneself. An accurate assessment of one's neighbor. Finally, an accurate assessment of God. Phillips Brooks, that elegant pulpiteer, once
said, "The true way to be humble is not to stoop until you
are smaller than yourself, but to stand at your real height
against some higher nature that will show you what the
real smallness of your greatness is."

"The real smallness of your greatness"; a phrase that
brings all down to scale, sets everyone in place. Not nec-
essarily in any crushing or overwhelming way. It can be

done most gently and lovingly; for humility—as Saint Paul tells us—is the fruit of love, the love that God is.

Jesus, on the night of his betrayal, not only taught but demonstrated the humility he seeks from all who would follow him. There was no servant in that upper room to wash the feet of the weary disciples as they entered for the Passover. And since none would stoop to take upon himself this lowly task, their Lord and Master, God Incarnate, Christ himself, took basin and towel and knelt at the feet of his friends. Then he said, "I have set you an example. As I have done to you, so you should do to others." An accurate assessment of God.

It boggles the mind. What an amazing condescension—in the best sense of that word—that God Almighty valued Peter and John, James too, and Andrew, as well as everyone who reads these words, as well as the one who writes them, enough to kneel and wash our dusty feet, in Jesus Christ, God-with-us, Emmanuel. What a power of humility was there! What a message of our own eternal value *and* the eternal value of our neighbor, those who sit beside us at the feast (including Judas the betrayer, for Judas's feet were washed as well).

Only one act, one gesture even more supreme, could illustrate and bring down to earth God's humility more completely. And that act occurred the following day, as the Lord of all creation, the One who gives us life, gave up his life; knew pain, rejection, death, the cosmic humiliation of the cross, that we might live.

And so we live. We live to choose his love and share that love in genuine humility; valuing ourselves as redeemed with a price, valuing our neighbors as those who share that same redemption, valuing and serving our God who has set before us such a rich inheritance.

What better words to draw all this together that those of Paul himself from his Epistle to the Philippians:

Let the same mind be in you that was in Christ Jesus,
    who, though he was in the form of God,
        did not regard equality with God
        as something to be exploited,
    but emptied himself,
        taking the form of a slave,
        being born in human likeness.
    And being found in human form,
        he humbled himself
        and became obedient to the point of death—
        even death on a cross.
    Therefore God also highly exalted him
        and gave him the name
        that is above every name.

                        —Philippians 2:5-9

Have *this* mind, this supremely humble mind, among yourselves. And Paul said,

> *Love is not . . . boastful or arrogant or rude.*

———— ✛ ————

Set us at the foot of your cross that we might see and know and recognize the full depth of your humility, the true price of our salvation. Convince us of our eternal worth, and teach us how to know that worth in others. Amen.

8

Of Grievances and Grudges

--- ☩

> *[Love] is not irritable or resentful.*
>
> *Do not fret over those who*
>   *prosper in their way,*
> *over those who carry out evil devices.*
> *Refrain from anger, and forsake wrath.*
> *Do not fret—it leads only to evil.*
>
> —Psalm 37:7-8

hus far things have been moving along quite nicely; even—dare I suggest?—relatively smoothly. The sentiments expressed have been moving; they have even, once in a while, stirred a passing pang of guilt, a stray trace of remorse; but it's all been rather distant, theoretical, and ideal. How many, after all, would ever actually claim to possess "the tongues of mortals and of angels"? Even those qualities of love Paul has traced—patience, kindness, lack of envy and boastfulness—are qualities any decent individual might say "Amen" to, might even claim a passing acquaintance with on one's best days. But in this verse we read that love is "not irritable or resentful." And, as the banker said when the pastor decided he had to preach on corporate investments, suddenly we've "quit preachin' and gone to meddlin.'"

"Not irritable or resentful"; that touches close to home. My wife informs me that even I get irritable. I simply reply that she's always saying that and that such comments make me very angry. It is as if someone had said to Paul, "Well, that's all very fine, all that Sunday morning stuff about love being this and not that, noble, kind, and such. But what about the world we live in for the rest of the week, where loving comes up against a brick wall? What about when love is not reciprocated but resisted, regarded with suspicion, hostility, even violence? What then?

It was Peter who posed the question: "How often *must* I forgive, Jesus? What are the guidelines, parameters, outer boundaries to this love idea of yours? You must have some; it can't go on forever. How about seven times; surely that's enough?" And Jesus told him, "Seventy times seven" (Matthew 18:22, RSV). And I'm sure he didn't mean we can quit at four hundred and ninety.

In saying that love "is not irritable or resentful," Paul is dealing with this question of the Christian's response to hurt, rejection, those "slings and arrows" not merely of "outrageous fortune" that Shakespeare's Hamlet must face but of even more outrageous other folk. And that is a question that must be answered almost every day; a question most of us are not answering very well. Let's look in more detail at what Paul proposes.

First, "love is not irritable." This would appear to constitute at most a minor sin, more a foible, a peccadillo. Irritability nowadays seems to be related more to the state of one's digestive system than to the destiny of one's immortal soul. Doesn't everyone have fits of touchiness, mini-explosions brought on, or touched off by the every-day ills, frustrations, annoyances of life? Surely this is nothing major, nothing to get upset, let alone scriptural about; nothing at all to merit inclusion in this soaring hymn to love.

Yet when all is said and done (and with irritability much more usually gets said than done), what is it that kills love? What is it that alienates and embitters daily life? What poisons relationships, devastates home life, withers marriages and covenants, shipwrecks friendships and partnerships? Is irritability not close to the heart of the problem? It's not so much the big things, the major crises and catastrophes, but the daily frictions—the silence here, sarcasm there, that can nibble away at love until it crumbles and collapses from within.

I remember reading news reports of a ship that went down in a storm off the Virginia coast. When the investigations were done, the reports all published, nothing major was to blame. The engines worked, the hull was sound, the navigation gear and radio did their job; the crew performed efficiently, even bravely. Yet that ship went to the bottom and took thirty-three lives. An accumulation of neglect—year after year of makeshift repairs, flimsy patches, and substandard replacement parts—caused shipwreck, catastrophe, and death.

Paul knew this. No one was more qualified to recognize all this, because Paul too was afflicted with a fiery temper. He had seen his own relationships disintegrate as a result of such minor disputes. And now he saw this young church at Corinth heading in the same disastrous direction. So he offers them the one thing that can save. He holds out again that gift of love: love that focuses not on the self—that tender, touchy, prickly cactus—but turns its focus out toward the other, toward the welfare and happiness of those around the self. For thus, and only thus, the time bomb—that unexploded mine at the center of existence—is defused; and friendship, trust, and mutuality can flourish again at the heart where they belong.

[Love] is not irritable.

Moving to the second point, Paul tells us love is not resentful; or as Willie Barclay puts it, love "does not store up the memory of every wrong it has received." What is resentment, after all, but irritation memorized, irritation transferred to the hard drive, copied to the long-term memory?

Barclay points out that the Greek word Paul uses here is basically an accountant's word. It means the act of entering items in a ledger. And this image evokes a nod of recognition. Who has not experienced that carefully maintained list of slights, grievances, and grudges that grows daily longer and ever more cherished each time its pages are scanned. Robert Burns, in his epic poem "Tam o' Shanter" has a splendid line as Tam sets out late at night from the pub to seek his way home:

> Where sits our sulky sullen dame,
> Gathering her brows like gathering storm,
> Nursing her wrath to keep it warm.

Now that's resentment!

And what a crippling thing it is! For resentment gets

a hold, a grip on someone; and the longer it is nursed, the stronger its grasp, until its victim is no longer in control. The ledger takes over.

Henry Drummond, in a brilliant flash, links this passage with the elder brother of the prodigal. There he stood outside the door, that honest, dutiful son, nursing his list of grievances against his spendthrift, wastrel brother, sulking in resentful rage, while inside the feast went on without him. He could not forget. He would not forgive. And thereby he sealed his own fate. He shut himself out from his father's house.

The situation at Corinth was similar. Different groups within that battered church had compiled their lists of grievances; many, maybe even all, legitimate to some extent. But because of these grievances they were cut off from one another; could no longer gather at the Lord's table, no longer hear the Word, share bread and wine, sense the one presence that might yet bring healing. Their lists had become walls, walls of sullen anger; and they were captive, imprisoned, barred from one another by resentment.

Jesus had another word for this when he said, "If any of you put a stumbling block before one of these little ones who believe in me, it would be better for you if a great millstone were fastened round your neck and you were drowned in the depths of the sea" (Matthew 18:6).

That is to say, as Drummond again points out, "it is the deliberate verdict of the Lord Jesus that it is better not to live than not to love."

The answer lies in love. Love is the power that can tear down those towering walls of heaped-up irritation; love that was "in Christ reconciling"—what a basic word that is!—"reconciling the world to himself . . . and entrusting the message of reconciliation to us" (2 Corinthians 5:19).

God has showed the way. For God too must have had lists—and what lists they were!—of grievances, failures, betrayals, broken vows, idolatries, atrocities going back as far as history and further. And yet, in Christ, God took those lists and tore them, shredded them page by bloodstained page. God destroyed them once for all time, canceled every one when we nailed Christ to a tree and his only prayer was, "Father, forgive them; for they do not know what they are doing" (Luke 23:34).

Where is there room for our resentment? If God, the just and righteous One, forgives and forgets; then who are we to keep our tawdry lists of petty hurts, to prolong them one day more? Here is the answer to the evils and pains we experience. Not to store them deep within as a perpetual source of hate and rage, a source that festers and infects the entirety of life—that's how people end up shooting random neighbors in the streets or planting car bombs. The secret is to accept the hurt, as Jesus did, to absorb it, and finally to forget. Only thus can we be liberated, set free for life and love again. The other way enslaves, binds our days into the dreary working out, passing on, and handing down, the multiplying of evil upon evil.

I once heard Hannah Arendt, a Jew who had to flee for life from the Nazis, say, "Forgiveness is the only way to reverse the irreversible flow of history."

Love is not irritable or resentful because, in the last analysis, resentment is a loser's game. It is the way of giving in to evil and the power of death, sharing their methods, joining their cause. Whereas the way of life, of Christ, the conquered, conquering Lord, is the royal way of love. In that way, though we stumble and fall, we may still get up and begin again as we seek to live in faith in a wintered world that yet is moving, slowly but steadily, toward spring.

———— ✠ ————

Lord, you know far better than we how we fail you; how many times the prison walls of anger and resentment rule our days. Deliver us, we pray. Deliver us through your gift of love; we cannot do it by ourselves. Then lead us toward that day of grace when we will be in Christ a new creation. Amen.

9

The Price of Forgiveness

────────────────────────────── ✛

[Love] is not irritable or resentful.

Bless the Lord, O my soul, . . . who forgives all your iniquity.

—Psalm 103:2

So my heavenly Father will also do to every one of you, if you do not forgive . . . from your heart.

—Matthew 18:35

e touched upon this tender, touchy, testing topic, the topic of forgiveness, in the previous chapter. As we examined Paul's words, "[Love] is not irritable or resentful," it became clear that this subject calls for a more extended treatment in a chapter of its own. My experience in preaching on forgiveness bears this out. Invariably I have been besieged after the sermon by a multitude of comments, questions, and suggestions.

So let us take another look at forgiveness, using a few vignettes to set the scene.

A husband, after months, perhaps years of infidelity and deception, decides one night to get the whole thing off his chest; to clear his uneasy conscience in one fell swoop. Perhaps the increasingly intricate web of lies and pretense has become too tangled. Perhaps his conscience has finally got the better of him. Perhaps someone has found out. For whatever reason, the man seizes the impulse and spells out names, dates, and sordid details to his unsuspecting spouse. And having done this, he feels immeasurably relieved, his aching burden lifted, his stained and guilty soul shriven and cleansed. He stands ready now to receive her understanding pardon. The wife is devastated.

A young and gravely wounded SS storm trooper, lying near death in an allied hospital in the final months of World War II, experiences a compelling desire to clear his conscience of his role in the massacre of Jewish refugees. Summoning the last of his resources, he gasps the whole thing out, crime by crime, to an American Jewish hospital orderly; then asks for absolution. He begs the man for pardon before he dies, for pardon in the name of the Jewish people.

A people experiences brutal slavery and then crushing racial and economic discrimination for centuries afterward. Finally after considerable pressure, the oppressors discover an ethical twinge or two and seek a conscience-salving word from their still not fully liberated victims.

Can forgiveness be too cheap? When and why and how should it be offered? Must it always be offered? Is forgiveness the appropriate, even the ethical, response in such situations as those outlined above?

Of all the traditional virtues, surely forgiveness is the most challenging, the most rewarding. It is an act that Jesus himself commended to his own heavenly Father as he prayed, "Father, forgive them; for they do not know what they are doing." Yet despite all this, forgiveness is no simple matter.

Cheap forgiveness is the issue; forgiveness that uses this holiest of virtues in a most unholy way, turning it into a way of avoiding the harsh reality of human failure and its consequences. "Escape-hatch forgiveness" we might call it—a forgiveness that denies responsibility for the past, ignores the need to make amends in the present, and refuses to project itself into changed ways for the future.

Such forgiveness remains willfully and selfishly blind to the depth and persistence of human pain; a pain that will not be shrugged off with a few words of apology, no matter how sincere the words may seem. What might be some of the implications of living with cheap forgiveness?

In the first place, this kind of forgiveness is, or can be, a denial of the one who sins against you. It can become a refusal to take that person and his or her offense seriously; an unwillingness to actually contend with that person, spelling out, in response to his or her confession, just what that wrong has done, the irreparable changes it has brought about.

Easy forgiveness can mean an unreadiness to descend to the grubby, tiresome level of daily life, where you work together with the offender to uncover how this evil came about, and what, if any, part you may have played—for complicity is much more a fact of life than most of us are ready to admit. "The recognition of complicity is the beginning of innocence"—as the poet Robert Penn Warren reminds us—and also the beginning of healing.

Cheap forgiveness signals an unwillingness to invest

the necessary energy to explore repentance and restoration—that painstaking, step-by-step rebuilding of relationship and trust through which genuine forgiveness may still be achieved. So cheap forgiveness denies, rejects, refuses to take seriously the full humanity of the offender, of the one who actually seeks forgiveness. And while such rejection may seem justified by the offense, it will rebound, not only upon the offender but upon the one offended against.

Second, cheap forgiveness also implies a denial, a drastic selling short of your own self; a rejection of the full humanity of the one asked to forgive. What you may be saying when you utter the words: "That's OK. Of course I forgive you. Forgive and forget" is not just that *he* doesn't count, that what she did is not worthy of serious attention. You are also saying something about yourself. You are expressing a cheapened view of your own integrity, a devalued sense of your personal worth as child of God.

In effect you are stating that you would rather accept the hurt and just forget it, which means for most of us bottling it up inside to fester and ferment. So you refuse to deal with the actual pain, the lasting hurt and offense, and you continue on through life as one of the multitude of walking wounded rather than as one healed and restored through the sacrament of reconciliation.

A third consequence of such facile forgiveness is a

failure to take God seriously, the denial of God's eternal claim on all of life. God's will for humanity is set forth in general outlines in the scriptures—the Sermon on the Mount, the Ten Commandments. God created us for this kind of life in community, trust, and peace.

When someone breaks God's laws, sowing mistrust, prejudice, and fear, and we respond by saying, "No problem. Don't get upset. Just say you're sorry and we'll forget the whole thing," we make a mockery of our teachings and traditions, all these time-honored and deadly serious structures set forth for human life and its survival in community. Our response is not unlike the cynical retort of the poet Heinrich Heine who, on his deathbed, is said to have remarked, "God will pardon me. That's [God's] business."

The healing communities of psychology and psychiatry have become increasingly aware of the cost of this denial. Karl Menninger's book *Whatever Happened to Sin?* is one sign of a renewed recognition that evil *does* exist, that right and wrong are not arbitrary social constructs but belong to the nature of reality. When we say "It doesn't matter" in the face of human evil; when we murmur in compassionate tones, "There but for the grace of God go I," we deny not only God and our own humanity, we actually destroy the moral fabric that makes us who we are.

Cheap forgiveness—this easy-going, relaxed, and apparently commendable attitude that permeates society today, is basically a denial. It denies the full humanity of the sinner, the offender. It denies the true integrity of the self, the one offended against. It denies the reality of God, who is the only source of authentic forgiveness.

What then are we to do? Do we need a new age of intolerance, a revival and affirmation of narrow, unforgiving attitudes? Perish that thought! What we must foster is the courage to tackle true forgiveness; to look again at the meaning of that New Testament term *repentance*, which according to the teachings of the faith is the one essential before *any* forgiveness is asked or given.

Repentance means a changed life. The Hebrew verb it comes from means "to turn"; repentance means to turn one's life around, to begin over again. It is not just a matter of muttering a swift apology, feeling a vague twinge of regret, and then continuing as before. Repentance entails an entirely new life in which the old ways are abandoned forever.

Yes, this concept *is* much more difficult, much tougher. But this is what sets apart true forgiveness, forgiveness that is shaped by our faith and modeled by our Savior, from all its imitations; those anything goes, nothing-really-matters attitudes that masquerade today as toleration. Forgiveness is not, never should, never can be easy. But when it is achieved, when true forgiveness happens, then love has found its fullness, true friendship is restored, and life, the abundant life that Jesus preached and lived, can flourish once again.

One final point: The Christian can never think or write about forgiveness without recalling the price Jesus paid for it, the crushing burden that he bore. If nothing else, surely this remembrance sets all our forgiving within its proper context.

Therefore we must handle Jesus' gift with care, with reverence, and with grateful joy. Thus may we rediscover God's forgiveness—no casual shrugging off of hurt, offense, or sin; but a tough, committed process of working things out together and in God's just and gracious sight. Then we will know forgiveness without limits that we read of in the Gospels, that we sing of in our hymns: God's amazing grace that can and will make all things new.

> There's a wideness in God's mercy
> like the wideness of the sea;
> There's a kindness in God's justice,
> Which is more than liberty.

———— ✚ ————

Teach true forgiveness, Lord. Set us before your cross that we may see the cost, hear the call, and come to know the tough, yet true deliverance that you offer us in Christ. Then bid us share with one another. Amen.

10

Don't Worry. Be Happy! But Be Careful!

☩

[Love] does not rejoice in wrongdoing, but rejoices in the truth.

hat do you rejoice at? I remember reading an asinine statement by a member of the British aristocracy to the effect that this world is divided into two kinds of people: those who treat their servants well, and those who do not. Let me suggest a somewhat different division of humanity: those who rejoice at wrong and those who rejoice at the right. Paul seems to suggest here that while the gospel *is* a source of rejoicing, it is vitally important that when we rejoice, we rejoice about the right things. Don't worry. Be happy! But be careful!

Two kinds of people. To begin with, what might Paul have in mind when he warns against rejoicing in wrongdoing? The New English Bible suggests a helpful approach when it translates 1 Corinthians 13:6, "Love . . . does not gloat over other [people's] sins." Love is not, for example, like Mrs. Candour, that character in Sheridan's *School for Scandal*, who is invariably candid, who makes a principle of scrupulously telling the truth—in as malicious and malevolent a manner as possible.

Yet if Paul's insight is accurate, there is at least a sliver of Mrs. Candour within most of us; a deeply concealed place where we could jump for glee when we discover something negative, detrimental, even scandalous about another human being.

It's not a very nice place. Indeed, if we ever stop to recognize it we're probably not proud of it at all. But it is there nonetheless; a part of our nature that wants to rejoice in learning evil of another. It is a complex, contorted sort of emotion; one made up of many components.

One such component is sheer relief that it is not oneself that is in trouble, that it is not one's own secret life that has been exposed to scandalized public gaze—at least not yet. A related facet is a sort of strategic satisfaction; strategic because such negative news about others can work overall to eliminate, or at least decrease, the competition. In this aggressive rat race of a world, when one contestant drops out or is temporarily disabled, that leaves a little more room for the rest of us.

Again, we take pleasure at someone else's misfortune because it shifts the focus; it diverts attention away from the potential discovery of *our* own faults. Indeed, if the bad news is "good" enough, our failings—those that are already known—may appear less serious, even trivial in comparison. What a golden opportunity to regain the advantage, to recultivate that essential sense of moral superiority: "I realize *I'm* not perfect, but did you hear the latest about . . . ?"

Finally I fear that we rejoice in others' wrongdoing because it's fun; because we humans are so constituted that we find a perverse pleasure in uncovering the weaknesses, the hidden wickednesses of another child of God. As someone wittily commented on Jesus' words: "It's so much easier to weep with those who weep than to rejoice with those who rejoice."

Jesus saw this. He ran up against it time after time in his confrontations with the religious authorities, the moral watchdogs of his day. When our Lord saw someone ill or in trouble, he moved immediately, almost instinctively, to bring relief, encouragement, and healing. His opponents, in contrast, could only ask, "What sin caused this? What can she have done? What is he being punished for? Is it even legal for her to be healed?"

Imagine the glee of that vindictive, bloodthirsty mob as they dragged the woman taken in adultery before Jesus. *Aha! At last we've got one. An indisputable sinner caught in the act. Just look at her! Look at the wretched creature, guilt all over her face.*

And Jesus did look at her. He looked at her face, gazed deep into her terrified eyes, and saw her fear, her shame, her humiliation. He saw too her repentance, her longing for another way of life. And he rejoiced at that; rejoiced to see such truth and blessedness; rejoiced to see his Father's full forgiving love already at work, already reflected there in her suddenly trusting, gentle eyes. "Woman, go your way, . . . and from now on do not sin again" (John 8:10, 11). And the truth that Jesus saw and rejoiced in in that woman's eyes knew victory that day over all those who gloried in her wrongdoing.

We see this rejoicing in the wrong in today's media, where bad news seems to be the only news fit to print. Even our churches, our denominations, and National and World Councils have been subjected to this treatment as "investigative journalists"—often with sharp axes of their own to grind—have uncovered perceived faults and failings. And to be sure, any institution, especially those of such broad scope and embrace, will make occasional mistakes. But instead of quietly and carefully pursuing truth, and rejoicing in such truth—the truth, for example, of the countless tons of emergency aid delivered by these fine institutions to the wretched and abandoned of this world—these naysayers search for a story that will sell, something to delight those who love to shake their heads and say, "Tut, tut!" from the sidelines. They try to make a buck, a buck at the expense of Christ, his church, and the poor he came to help.

So much of what we read in the newspapers or view on TV is a rejoicing in the wrong, a pandering to the common, yet regrettable, human impulse to savor and find entertainment in the disasters of others. I worry about the callousness this fosters in society.

I think of the great metropolis in which I carry out my ministry and of the way New York City is presented by the media—a place of crime and violence, of dirt, of despair and degradation, of collapsing social structures, and of mounting intolerance. And all these things are true in part. Yet they are only *part* of the story.

The other part tells of a city in which people from all backgrounds, races, cultures, languages, lifestyles, age, and economic groupings live together in reasonable harmony and peace, most of the time. The city *is* a difficult testing place; yet multitudes of individuals succeed in living here and even in doing so with grace and generosity. It's a miracle that such a vast, complex, and intensely lived-in place works at all. But what one reads and sees, most of the time, is a rejoicing in the wrong with little or no mention of the right.

A curious thing about the Greek Paul uses in this verse. The second time he uses that verb *rejoice*, he modifies it so that it literally reads, "[Love] rejoices *with* the right." Might Paul be indicating that the Christian who seeks love, who makes love the guiding principle, will search out those elements of good, of truth, of promise, within every situation; and then will not merely rejoice at, but *with* those elements? In other words, rather than simply noting, or reporting the presence of the good, we must be joining ourselves to it, becoming ourselves a living part and partner of the good, and thus encouraging it to grow, to prosper, and to triumph over wrong.

As everyone knows, the pessimist sees the glass half-empty, while the optimist sees it half-full. There was a marriage in the little rural town of Cana, and in the midst of the rejoicing the wedding wine ran out. And while the guests were staring at those empty flasks, complaining, perhaps secretly rejoicing at the wrong—"How embarrassed they must be! What humiliation! What a scandal!"—while the guests saw only empty jugs, Jesus' eyes were fixed on those brimming vats of water. And through them he worked a miracle that brought joy to every heart.

I heard someone recently talking about Stonehenge

and discussing various attempts to unfold its mystery. The speaker said an intriguing thing: "Stonehenge is like a mirror. It doesn't so much tell you about the past, as it reflects back the preconceptions you brought with you." But this is also true of life. What we see depends on what we look for.

I'm reminded of an old, dear friend, caught up with all her being in that dreadful daily battle against cancer. When Sarah walks into the oncologist's waiting room the place is irresistibly transformed—changed from a mortuary-in-waiting into a living community of personalities; individuals who share similar problems and fears and also similar hopes and dreams, loves and laughter. When I complimented her once about her infectiously positive attitude she responded, " It's just as easy to be cheerful as to be dismal all day. It takes no more effort to be positive and joyful, and it sure feels a whole lot better."

We can go through life rejoicing at the wrong; criticizing, analyzing, poking holes in possibilities, laughing cynically at other people's failures. There's no lack of material, that's for sure! But what kind of life, what kind of fun, what kind of long-term satisfaction lies in this approach? What kind of rejoicing will there be if such cynics are proved right, and this world goes down the tubes?

On the other hand, by rejoicing *with* the right, rejoicing with the truth of God we find in Christ, and then joining our rejoicing to that of others in a company of hope that seeks to bring rejoicing wherever there is loneliness and despair; by rejoicing in God's right we will find life. We will find a life that is abundantly worth living, a life that knows and shares God's genuine rejoicing; a rejoicing that begins right now and stretches throughout eternity.

[Love] does not rejoice in wrongdoing, but rejoices in the truth.

———— ✢ ————

Teach us to know the honest joy that comes, not from ignoring or hiding from the wrongs and evils of this world but from believing in and sharing in your triumph over wrong, from setting our own lives within that vast conspiracy of grace that begins at the cross and yet will storm the gates of hell, will lead into the glorious kingdom of your love. Amen.

11

Will You Still Need Me?

━━━━━━━━━━━━━━━━━━━━━━━━━━━

[Love] bears all things, believes all things, hopes all things, endures all things.

ashion, particularly where I reside—not far from Manhattan's Fashion Mile and Garment District—is evidently a fickle thing. This observation is based on more than the wandering height of hemlines or the contours of a pair of slacks. Fashion, with all its fickleness, reaches into every facet of life; even into such areas as the moral virtues—those universally commended personal characteristics, standards of behavior and propriety. In character, as well as in clothing, humankind is subject to trends and fads.

For example, consider this epitaph discovered in an English country churchyard by Rita Snowden, the distinguished New Zealand churchwoman and author. The headstone reads, "Vicar of this parish for forty years, without ever showing the least sign of enthusiasm." I wonder what the folk who carved that message were trying say about this revered old gentleman when they memorialized his lack of enthusiasm.

As I thought about this chapter's text: "Love bears, . . . believes, . . . hopes, . . . endures all things," it struck me that they may well have been saying that from their point of view—that of a village congregation in England's green and timeless hills—endurance counted for a great deal more than enthusiasm.

Consider the story of Isaac and Rebekah. Abraham sends his trusted steward to the ancestral homeland. His task is to find a suitable wife for Isaac—the promised child of the covenant. After many adventures, Rebekah is found and persuaded to return to become Isaac's bride.

> Isaac went out in the evening to walk in the field; and looking up he saw camels coming. And Rebekah looked up, and when she saw Isaac, she slipped quickly from the camel, and said to the servant, "Who is the man over there, walking in the field to meet us?" The servant said, "It is my master." So she took her veil and covered herself. And the servant told Isaac all the things that he had done. Then Isaac brought her into his mother Sarah's tent.

He took Rebekah, and she became his wife; and he loved her. So Isaac was comforted after his mother's death.

—Genesis 24:63-67

A picturesque and charming tale. But note the sequence at the close. Isaac brought Rebekah into the tent and took her as his wife; then and *only* then, we are told that he loved her. And the love of Isaac and Rebekah is remembered to this day.

What is love? Not only traditionally accepted love—between a man and a woman—but love as our society is being challenged to redefine it, love between two mature, consenting adults. What constitutes love? How does it begin? How may it be fostered, encouraged to endure?

Certainly today we place the emphasis on enthusiasm—that giddy first infatuation—romantic love. Many of us were reared on it through movies and musicals, plays, TV series. "Falling in love" we call it; and it *is* a marvelous, magical, gloriously enthusiastic experience.

But what about endurance? What about those divorce statistics, so shocking and sad I've given up looking for fear I'll swear off weddings altogether! What about a society of broken homes and abandoned children, single parents, multiple sex partners, sexually transmitted disease, lonely and hurting lives?

What happens when the person you love doesn't love you anymore? Where does all that enthusiasm go as the years wear on? "Will you still need me?" asked the Beatles. And as one grows older, their question grows more poignant and painful. What is love? How *can* it endure?

First of all love *is*, in part, enthusiasm. Falling in love, infatuation, physical desire, all the raptures, swoons, and crazily wonderful impulses that poets have celebrated since the dawn of time; love *is* all of that. And without all of that, life would be colder, bleaker, much more barren. But this enthusiasm of love is fleeting, evanescent. One simply cannot survive in a perpetual state of such exaltation, such sheer enthusiasm.

What then? Must we fall out of love and move on to someone else, someplace else, to begin the cycle all over again? Or might there be a way to move along, to progress *within* love, to advance to something stronger, more complete; a love that bears, believes, hopes, *and* endures?

One finds this kind of love in the scriptures. "The love . . . of long intimacy," is what the *Interpreter's Dictionary of the Bible* calls it. This is a love which—as the dictionary describes it—"includes the sexual dimension, but is not comprised of it. . . . It is rather the intimate devotion and loyalty of life together." Amazing what you find in a Bible dictionary!

Loyalty, mutuality, responsibility; these also are components of enduring love. Forgiveness too—one should never try to make it without forgiveness—God's love surely demonstrated that as it took shape in Jesus, gave itself completely in his life, death, and resurrection; in his amazing, saving grace.

Here are the ingredients of true and lasting love. Love bears all things. In any continuing, loving relationship there are things which have to be borne, to be put up with simply because we are human. We have our faults, our selfish ways, our hurtful and thoughtless habits established over many decades, many failures and refusals to communicate. And there's only so much change that even the most flexible are capable of in one lifetime. Love bears all things.

Love believes all things. This does not mean that one must be totally gullible. Accepting lie after lie, evasion after evasion; tolerating continual physical or emotional abuse; here is no foundation for any kind of love. This is, in fact, not love at all, for such tolerance can only encourage the worst in the beloved.

It is a different matter to believe *in* the other person; to invest oneself in and work hard to support the very best that he or she can become. People tend to become what we expect them to be. If a teacher believes a child is stupid, that child swiftly learns to respond stupidly. And the process does not end with childhood. Love is all about believing, believing the very best possible of one another. Only thus do we allow that possibility to become a fully living, loving actuality. Love believes all things.

Love hopes all things. Love goes *on* hoping—even after twenty, thirty years together—it continues to look forward with high and holy expectation of a richer, stronger love to come. Love hopes all things.

Love endures all things. And this is the toughest claim. There are marriages, relationships that have deteriorated to a point where their perpetuation means to prolong a living hell. As a counselor with over thirty years' experience of love's festivals and battle lines, I realize that a time may come when our human love cannot, must not put up with anymore.

But Paul writes of a love *beyond* our own; a love he holds up as goal but also as promise. This is God's love, a consummate love toward which ours must move and strive. Yet at the same time, God's love is there already, waiting for us, if we will only ask. Even when our own frail loves give way to failure and defeat, God's love endures. We may rest secure in this.

The Scottish hymn writer, George Matheson, knew this experience at least as well as anyone who ever lived, who ever loved. Matheson was engaged to marry someone he had loved long and deeply, but when his doctors informed him that he was soon to lose his sight, she left him, and his dreams lay in the dust. He was plunged into severe depression, only to find, right in the darkest abyss, the strong, pure light of another love. This was a fuller love, a love that held him firm and would *not* relinquish its hold. Out of that experience, Matheson wrote the hymn that has brought comfort and hope to countless believers.

> O Love that wilt not let me go,
> I rest my weary soul in thee;
> I give thee back the life I owe,
> That in thine ocean depths its flow
> May richer, fuller be.
>
> O Light that followest all my way,
> I yield my flickering torch to thee;
> My heart restores its borrowed ray,
> That in thy sunshine's blaze its day
> May brighter, fairer be.
>
> O Joy that seekest me through pain,
> I cannot close my heart to thee;
> I trace the rainbow thru the rain,
> And feel the promise is not vain,
> That morn shall tearless be.
>
> O Cross that liftest up my head,
> I dare not ask to fly from thee;

> I lay in dust life's glory dead,
> And from the ground there blossoms red
> Life that shall endless be.

That strong, enduring love is available today. It is a love that bears with us, believes in us, hopes for us, endures despite us. It is a love that will never let us go but will go with us into every care and challenge as a gift of grace to all we meet, as the rock-firm core of all relationships, and as a sure, abiding joy that endures within our hearts.

Let your love sustain our love and lead us toward that which will endure. Amen.

12

The Beginning of the End

⊕

Love never ends. But as for prophecies, they will come to an end; as for tongues, they will cease; as for knowledge, it will come to an end.

ike 1 Corinthians 13 itself, this book has three sections. Chapters 1–4 dealt with "The Necessity of Love." We examined Paul's conviction that *without love* all other gifts—tongues, faith, knowledge, self-sacrifice—were utterly worthless.

Chapters 5–11 identified "The Qualities of Love," and we looked at Paul's analysis of love's many facets and dimensions. Thus we studied how love is patient, kind, not envious, irritable, or resentful.

This chapter, "The Beginning of the End," opens the

third and final section, which we might call "The Endurance of Love"; a section in which Paul argues that love outlasts everything; that love is, indeed, the one thing that never ends.

Seated one day at the keyboard—it was the Tuesday before Holy Week, about eleven in the morning—suddenly, out of the blue or wherever else such disasters leap from, my computer screen went blank, and I was confronted with the following chilling message: Operating System Missing

Needless to say I went out of my mind. Trusting in the Lord is all very well in situations of extreme temptation, even dire persecution for the faith, but it seems to me highly suspect that there is not one word in this great book the Bible about whom to call upon when your operating system is missing.

Don't bother—please refrain from writing or calling to inform me that I should have kept backups. Doesn't everyone keep backups after all or at least intend to at the earliest oportunity? Anyway, there I was, with sermons, poetry, prayers, lectures, book manuscripts—ten years of the stuff—stored away; backed up, yes, but backed up in a place I could no longer get into.

I sometimes wonder about Albert Einstein, and what would have happened if computers had come along just fifty years earlier. There he sits at the console, weary from weeks of high-powered deduction, all of which now draws to its climax. The screen reads E=mc. Then instead of punching in a 2, the exhausted genius groggily hits a colon, and the entire theory of relativity is gone, vanished down the tubes of forever and forever. Amen.

I know it probably couldn't happen. I'm sure a host of computer folks could pounce on me and explain exactly *why* it couldn't happen. But it happened to me that Tuesday before Holy Week; and believe me, a thing like that can induce a sizeable feeling of transience, a most powerful conviction of the fleetingness of things.

What is there that endures? In this global economy where people's livelihoods and whole industries are wiped out by the fluctuating price of a barrel of crude or the future value of the yen; in this world where people's homes vanish overnight in hurricane, flood, and fire; where massive public buildings are vulnerable to relatively tiny bombs; where marriage and family, once the center of stability and continuity, are about as permanent as this year's wardrobe; in a world and time like this, what endures? What is there to hold onto?

I read recently Martin Gilbert's superbly written biography of Winston Churchill. It is a gripping tale, for all its 900-plus pages, a tale of drama and adventure. Yet one thing struck me again and again. In those times, some fifty years ago, when I was just about the age of the youngsters in our cherubs' choir, Great Britain was a vast world power. With her colonies and dominions she laid claim to one quarter of this globe. Yet in a few short years, having triumphed in the most massive conflict ever fought, her power was spent. And now history passes her by.

What do they think when they look, *if* they look at this, those mighty ones in Congress, those world leaders who strut the podiums of power and talk of being a chosen people of manifest destiny? Do they believe they are somehow exempt—different from the Brits, the Romans, Egyptians, Babylonians, who all believed the self-same thing?

> Far-called, our navies melt away;
>> On dune and headland sinks the fire:
> Lo, all our pomp of yesterday
>> Is one with Nineveh and Tyre!
> Judge of the Nations, spare us yet,
>> Lest we forget—lest we forget!

So warned that poet of empire, Rudyard Kipling in his poem "Recessional "

So we search amid this impermanent world for something that endures. We invest in gold, treasury bills, real estate, trying to keep one step ahead of the whirlpool flux of economics. We attempt to guide our children into jobs that the madness of the marketplace will not eliminate. We seek full, honest relationships to carry us beyond the latest craze—the newest, brightest paperback on the psycholiterary scene. We turn our minds toward learning, wanting to produce something of lasting benefit: some theory or concept, work of art, or new invention that will survive at least beyond our own allotted span.

Yet over all this yearning hangs the shadow of our century with its mushroom clouds and killing fields, its overpopulation and mass starvation, its looming ecological disasters. Behind it all we hear that steady, unrelenting voice that murmurs: *What's the use?* It used to be that mothers would reassure their children in the night by telling them, "Hush, child! There's nothing to be afraid of." Today that message often wears a different emphasis, asserting that there *is* nothing, and "nothing" is a state very much to be afraid of.

> *As for prophecies, they will come to an end; as for tongues, they will cease; as for knowledge, it will come to an end.*

That dusty little caravan—that tiny, insignificant parade winding its way around the hills and valleys toward the Jerusalem city gates—how laughable it must have seemed to those with any reason to assume that they themselves or the institutions they belonged to were likely to endure.

The Roman soldiers, on sentry duty at the gates or glancing from the shady doorway of their guardroom to inquire what all this dust and din was raised by; what did they think as they glimpsed Jesus on his donkey, being hailed with conquering swords of palm leaf as he entered the holy city? "Another Jew-boy prophet from the hills, no doubt. Another young, well-meaning country bumpkin, full of tired ideas he thinks are new as dew upon this morning's gardens; and ready, ripe as a falling fig, to be bought off, co-opted by the holy ones, or jailed and crucified by some of us. Poor sucker!"

The priests and law-abiding Pharisees, craning from the rear of the throng or gazing down from windows high in the ancient walls; saying in their pious, brittle tones, "This agitation must be stopped. It's the old countryside Messiah scene again; this time from Galilee, of all places. If something isn't done, our hard-won compromise with Rome, the privileged position of the faith itself, may be imperiled. Yes, it would be nice to wait, to let this nuisance fizzle out in its own time; but who can afford that risk? For their own sake the people must be led to seek his elimination, his execution."

No doubt there were the wise ones too, the erudite scripture scholars who, as they peered out from their libraries at the rabble in the streets, would wag their beards and tut-tut at this foolhardy new example of enthusiasm. "Why can't these uncouth, uneducated, masses realize they are impeding the path of wisdom and behave themselves before it is too late?"

And while the empire, the church, the academy—those enduring institutions of this world—were muttering in outrage or in scorn, the Son of Man and Son of God rode by in lowly pomp toward his death.

"What is there that endures?" the ages ask. And in reply the rich old tale begins again as a young country-carpenter-turned-preacher rides a donkey through the gates of proud Jerusalem. What is there that endures? Follow him through his Holy Week, through our anything but Holy Week. Stand among the crowd as he purges the temple, heals the sick, disputes with the authorities. Sit close around a table in an upper room and share a loaf, a cup in the encroaching darkness. Kneel with him in a garden; then kneel again beneath a cross that bears the bitter weight of all of human tragedy and human hope. Then tread at dawn the path to the Easter garden. Stand before that vacant, conquered tomb. Hear the words that will be spoken there. And see if, in all your transience, you can discover for yourself what it is that will endure, endure until the end of time and then beyond.

———— ✛ ————

Take all our longing—our search for something permanent and lasting we can build upon—and focus them around the life and death and resurrection of the Christ. Lead us to the cross. Let us feel its crushing weight on all our pride, our hopes, our little dreams. Then guide us beyond into the garden; the garden where it all begins and ends, and ever is and shall be, world without end. Amen.

13

Through a Glass Darkly

For now we see through a glass, darkly.
   —1 Corinthians 13:12, KJV

But this is your hour, and the power of darkness.
   —Luke 22:53

he following meditation—set in the mind of one of the disciples in hiding on Holy Saturday—recalls thoughts, feelings, fears, as they set out only two days before to walk toward Gethsemane in the darkness.

The night was very dark.
Clouds must have drifted in, blotted out
the brightness of the Nisan moon of Passover.

You could hardly see your hand before your face,
I recall, and as we left that Upper Room,
regained the narrow street and then set off toward
the Mount Of Olives shadows seemed to settle in,
fall into place beside us.
We walked amid a growing throng of shadows.
Yes, the night was very dark.

Hard it was, you realize,
to tell just where this blackness came from;
whether these were shadows of the night
or of the mind and heart. We looked at one another,
and it was as if we saw through darkened lenses.
We looked ahead at him—our Lord and Leader -
and a murkiness crept in upon our sight.

Was it the gloom of ignorance we felt?
For we had thought, at last,
that things were moving full ahead,
that Jesus really had a plan
not just to save his life and ours
but to redeem the land, to bring back Holy Israel
from the dark obscure into the light of freedom,
independence from the pagan heel of Rome.
We had thought his entry into Jerusalem
with cheering crowds, cries of "Messiah!,"
flailing palms, would signify the time of acclamation,
his coming at the last into his kingdom and his reign.

We had hoped that we, his closest friends
and followers, would have a role in all of this,
would find a space within the new regime,
would know after the months and years of hardship
—traveling the dusty roads and villages
with nothing but the clothes we wore,
the sandals on our feet—
that we would meet at last our due reward,
could count on places by his side
when he assumed the throne that he had moved
toward across these hard and testing years.

Our minds, you see, were shadowed,
somehow darkened by the hopes we had been born with,
so that we only saw the freedom we had hoped for;
could not even glimpse the fuller, truer liberty
he lived out by our side and in our company.
We heard his teaching, hung on his every word,
or so we thought, and yet these words
passed through a filter, took on darkness
from the shade within our minds.
And so we saw him only, as it were,
"through a glass darkly."

There was another darkness
dogged our footsteps on that walk.
It was the dark of fear,
the sheer deep pit of terror

opening again before our feet, behind our backs,
as we remembered his last words at the supper table,
words of being broken and poured out;
as our reluctant, sluggish minds
yet insisted on connecting words like these
with other sayings spoken here and there
amid the conversations on the road;
shocking words about a cross, and suffering,
about a death that must be taken up, lived through;
even worse, about such things waiting also
for his followers, if they were true to him.
We used to disregard such talk, set it aside,
tried our very hardest to forget such things,
to hide from them. But then that night
the whole idea came home again to roost,
like a recurring nightmare,
when Judas left so strangely
just before the broken bread, the cup.
Why did we glance about so nervous as we left,
scurry across the open spaces, utter scarce one word
as we approached the place, Gethsemane?
Why did we huddle silent in the cover of the bushes,
fail to join him in his prayers, then fall asleep
like weary wandered sheep from sheer exhaustion
so that when he was arrested we were only half awake?
We were afraid.

The darkened blind of fear
had been drawn down upon our timid souls
and we could see him only, as it were,
"through a glass darkly."

An even deeper dark was there,
a blackness hard to spell out even to oneself,
yet hanging like a pall across what happened on that night.
Not only ignorance and fear were there, but sin itself—
that twisted serpent "self"—had entered in
and spread its deadly poison into all we thought
and saw and did. You see, if this, then, was the end:
if these sounds of marching feet,
calling voices on the wind,
clashing swords and spears,
flashing torches in the distance,
meant that he must face defeat,
must now taste the bitter failure of his vision,
the full weight of the revenge of the authorities;
then it's "every man for himself."
"Maybe this darkness is a friend after all.
Maybe there is still one chance to creep away,
escape the Roman net and get back home again to Galilee,
refuge with my family and friends."
So we thought; and we all fled.
We joined that darkness which had pressed us all around,
gave ourselves to its embrace,

and in ignorance and fear and love of self
abandoned him and all we held most dear,
ran for our miserable lives
and now are gathered here to mourn
and ask each other, "Why?"

The whole thing seemed to happen,
don't you see, in the pitch dark, among deep shadows.
What was it he said to them again?
"But this is your hour and the power of darkness."
Shadows surround us still. It is as if
we have been living in a darkened world of late.
And while we gather here and wait,
not knowing what or who it is we wait for,
we all share a sense of seeing everything
as if it were perceived, "through a glass darkly."

———— ✠ ————

14

The End of the Beginning

And now faith, hope, and love abide, these three; and the greatest of these is love.

he scene is a hilltop somewhere in Russia. A desperate group of convicted conspirators and thieves is being driven by former friends and fellow partisans toward the edge of a cliff, where they are to be executed for their crimes. One of them, Galuzin—barely more than a schoolboy as Pasternak describes him in *Doctor Zhivago*—falls on his knees as he scrambles backward with the rest, and cries out:

Forgive me, comrades, I'm sorry, I won't do it again, please let me off. Don't kill me. I haven't lived yet. I want to live a little longer, I want to see my mother just once more. Please let me off, comrades, please forgive me, I'll do anything for you. I'll kiss the ground under your feet. Oh help, help, Mother, I'm done for!

A volley of twenty shots, discharged at some inaudible command, mowed down half the condemned, killing most of them outright. Another salvo finished off the rest. The boy Terioshka Galuzin twitched longest, but finally he too lay still.

A heartrending, most *un*likely scene to begin the final chapter of a book on Paul's immortal "Hymn to Love." Yet a scene that, with others from literature, art, and drama, forms an archetype, an overarching image that haunts this twentieth century as it draws toward a close. It is the image of violent, relentless, and meaningless death.

Each morning's headlines serve up their own regular confirmation of this bleak, compelling symbol. It is carved into the changing-yet-unchanging faces of atrocity across the decades—the Brown Shirts, SS, and the KGB, those Central and South American death squads, the Cambodian Khmer Rouge, Serbian ethnic cleansers, Rwanda's tribal slaughterers. We glimpse its chilling features in the hostage-takers, car-jackers, terror-bombers, random-killers, those continual reminders of the Holocaust. Add to these the random, yet incessant demands of natural disaster; of earthquake, hurricane, fire, and flood, and the resulting picture is that of violent, relentless, meaningless death.

In a speech at MIT in 1949 Winston Churchill looked back to the year 1900, "Little did we guess that what has been called The Century of the Common Man would witness, as its outstanding feature, more common men killing each other with greater facilities than in any other five centuries put together in the history of the world."

In face of this, what *is* there that endures? Amid all the transience, the savagery, and meaninglessness of our time, where can one hope to find abiding values; something to build a life, a home, a family, even a destiny upon?

One reads the paper, scans the daily diet of disease, disaster, and despair and feels an impulse to get out; to pack up and skip this explosive society, to seek refuge in some unspoiled corner of the world. During their latter years my parents knew such dreams as they visited that idyllic land called Yugoslavia. After World War II, several British families sought a peaceful, if isolated, life in the South Atlantic in the remoteness of the Falkland Islands. One feels the impulse to get out, but where can one escape to?

Over against all of this death, what does this love Paul writes to the Corinthians about have to offer? Is our faith merely an enchanted fairy tale of immortality, a gracefully adapted springtime legend of the nature cycle? Birth once again succeeding death? The eternal bright return of daffodils, the butterfly's emerging from the chrysalis? Is this our answer to this world, this valley of dry bones in which we live?

Suppose we look a little further at the Easter message. Suppose we dare to peer behind the banks of lilies, beneath the lore and legend, to look back at the Gospel narratives themselves.

What we find there is certainly not the customary stuff of fairy tale. It begins with a parade, to be sure, but things swiftly degenerate. They descend in a rush to a betrayal, the selling of a life for silver, the cowardice of followers and common folk, a rigged and hasty trial with a verdict based on politics and fear, and then a public execution, not all that different from the one Pasternak describes—the victims flogged, driven to a high place, and nailed up for death.

It does end in a garden. Yet that garden is in fact a cemetery; a place of skulls and dust, inscriptions, coffins, mounds of heavy earth. Hardly the typical setting for a happy-ever-after. No, the Easter message—the entire narrative of Holy Week—is no altogether-lovely fairy tale. These Gospel narratives, for all their confusion here and there, their differing versions, conflicting testimonies along the way, bear the sharp taste of reality, seem rooted in the self-same stuff—the bloody, agonizing stuff we read of and despair about each day: betrayal, brutality, the gallows, and the grave.

What then is this Easter story in its stark reality telling us? Is it simply stating that a long, long time ago someone is reported to have returned from the dead? If that were all it would not be enough. Lazarus already did that in the Gospels; even in our own time we read such reports.

Perhaps Paul gets as close to the inner core of these events as any when he writes,

And now faith, hope, and love abide, these three; and the greatest of these is love.

Love it is that endures, endures above all else. Love never ends, even though we human folk resent it, reject it, pin it—pin the love of God in Jesus—up on a piece of criss-crossed wood to bleed and die. Even then it will not, cannot cease to be itself but prays in that supremely loving prayer, "Father forgive them, for they do not know not what they are doing."

Even though we slay God's love, leave it cold and buried in the tomb, death will not, cannot hold it. The grave cannot contain the power that created it, that created life *and* death. Our Lord returns and *yet* returns to woo us to the end of time, to woo us with the miracle of God's undying love.

What is there that endures, that never ends? Love endures; the most precious, even though it seems the most fragile and vulnerable of gifts. It is a gift that moves among us, lives in our relationships with children, parents, spouses, lovers, friends; even churches, communities, and nations. Yet it is, at the same time, uncontrollable, uncon-fineable, impossible to possess, preserve, ensure for one-self. Love is that radiant, tender gift that never will be fully ours; yet it is the one thing that endures, that endures in us, through us, and for us.

There is no way we can hold it, clasp it, own it. But if we will release our grasp and give ourselves, entrust ourselves, give ourselves away, then love can take its hold and bear us. It will not bear us away or deliver us from all pain, but it will carry us *through* pain, secure within God's everlasting arms.

What is it that people fear most about death? When you get right down to it, as I so often am compelled to do in my calling, it is not chiefly the pain. Nor is it the unknown that people dread. It is, for most at least, the separation; the loss of all they love. Then Easter's word is: "Fear no more! It is love that endures. And love means reunion, reconciliation, the reuniting and perfection—at the last—of all that now is unfulfilled, of all our earthly, partial and as-yet-imperfect loves."

One final tale, also set on a hilltop and within the

wide embrace of human tragedy, as was Zhivago's. Elam Davies—that bard of the pulpit—ended his farewell sermon at Fourth Presbyterian in Chicago with this reminiscence from his native Wales. It was an evening of glowing sunset and he and his wife had driven to the top of a local Welsh landmark to catch the spectacular display. All God's kaleidoscope was spread before them like a cosmic artist's canvas, when they noticed an old, battered car pull in alongside. An elderly couple emerged and moved to the rear doors where lay their son of later years, a child full grown, yet physically so incapacitated he could not sit up on the seat.

Somehow the two of them contrived—great effort combined with gentleness—to slide his legs around and hold him at the door facing out, but he could not lift his head. Then: "Just as the sun in all it's magnificence was to give its final burst of glory, as if God were dazzling us by the pyrotechnics of the universe, they put their finger—the father did and the mother a little later—under this young man's chin and just pointed him out there. And I knew, at that very moment I knew that God can dazzle us with all the magnificence of God's universe; but that the secret of the universe, the *heart* of the universe, was revealing its glory altogether, not in the sunset by all means altogether but in the compassion, grace, and love that comes to us when we need it most and says, 'There it is. There it is. And there, my boy, you are. And you matter

. . . you *matter*.'" Two hilltop scenes—one of terror, one of tenderness. Which will it be?

That valley of dry bones described by Ezekiel the prophet—a place of random, relentless, and meaningless death—will history end up there, in the bone yard? "Why didn't the skeleton cross the road, Daddy?" My daughter Nicola's fourth-grade joke that has stuck with me ever since. And the response, "Because it didn't have the guts."

Do we? Can we—the twentieth-century heirs of that bewildered band on Easter morn—of that feuding, factious fellowship in Corinth, not merely read and sing and say that love endures but begin to live it, act it, share it?

"Why do you look for the living among the dead?" asked the angel at the tomb. Will people say this of the Christians of today? Do people see in us just another valley of historic, perhaps elegant, but exceedingly dry bones? Or do we have the guts after all; the guts to be God's Easter risen people?

Pierre Teilhard de Chardin, the French priest-anthropologist-theologian penned these visionary words about our future:

> The day will come when, after harnessing the ether, the winds, the tides, gravitation, we shall harness for God the energies of love. And, on that day, for the second time in the history of the world, [humanity] will have discovered fire.

Take my eyes, O God, and see through them.
Take my lips, and speak through them.
Take my days, and live through them.
Take my heart, and set it on fire. Amen.